T0209362

A Rape of the Soul so Profound

As Aborigines began to sicken physically and psychologically, they were hit by the full blight of the alien way of thinking. They were hit by the intolerance and uncomprehending barbarism of a people intent only on progress in material terms, a people who never credited that there could be cathedrals of the spirit as well as of stone . . . It is my belief that Aboriginal Australia underwent a rape of the soul so profound that the blight continues in the minds of most blacks today.

[Kevin Gilbert]

A Rape of the Soul so Profound

The Return of the Stolen Generations

Peter Read

Routledge
Taylor & Francis Group

LONDON AND NEW YORK

For J.M.A.
In gratitude

First published 1999 by Allen & Unwin

Published 2020 by Routledge
2 Park Square, Milton Park, Abingdon, Oxon OX14 4RN
605 Third Avenue, New York, NY 10017

Routledge is an imprint of the Taylor & Francis Group, an informa business

National Library of Australia
Cataloguing-in-Publication entry:

Read, Peter, 1945–.
    A rape of the soul so profound: the return of the
    stolen generations.

    Bibliography.
    Includes index.
    ISBN 1 86448 885 9.

    1. Link-up. 2. Aborigines, Australian—Families. 3. Family
    reunions—Government policy—Australia. 4. Aborigines,
    Australian—Treatment. 5. Aborigines, Australian—Removal.
    6. Aborigines, Australian—Child welfare. 7. Aborigines,
    Australian—Government policy. I. Title.

362.849915094

Set in 11/13 pt Goudy Old Style by DOCUPRO, Sydney

ISBN-13: 9781864488852 (pbk)

Contents

Acknowledgments   vi
Preface   vii
Prologue: The Stolen Generations: Who are we?   ix

1 The oral evidence   1
2 The written evidence   17
3 The Stolen Generations   46
4 'Like being born all over again': the establishment
   of Link-Up   71
5 'I don't mix with Aboriginals, you know': working
   with Link-Up clients   101
6 At the edge of the firelight: coming home, partly   124
7 Calling in the accounts   150
8 Sorry Business   166
9 In the courts: 'In the middle of the ocean,
   drowning'   188

Bibliography   211
Endnotes   216
Index   229

Acknowledgments

The author is grateful to the following publishers who have consented to allow the material in this book to be republished:

Viking Books, *Overland*, Aboriginal History Inc., Transworld Publishers, Link-Up (NSW) Aboriginal Corporation, the Institute for Aboriginal Development, the NSW Ministry of Aboriginal Affairs and the Humanities Research Centre ANU.

I am particularly grateful to Joy Williams for the use of some photographs previously unpublished and for our continuing conversations, to an anonymous referee, to John Iremonger for his perceptive comments on rearranging the material, and to my editor David Horton who, through laborious and thoughtful use of the 'cut' and 'paste' buttons, re-organised the manuscript and revealed to me the whole work in a new and constructive light.

Preface

Since the 1970s I have worked both as a historian of Aboriginal Australia and for a time as an employee of Link-Up (NSW). The writings in this book are drawn from articles, interviews, pamphlets and submissions which I wrote between 1976 and 1998. All concern, in various ways, those Aboriginal people who were removed from their families while children and raised apart from their communities and their Indigenous inheritance.

Since almost all the pieces here were written for particular purposes, they have been altered to varying degrees to make them relevant to the present book. None appears exactly in its original form, while others have been altered substantially, added to and subtracted from to create a more coherent narrative and to avoid repetition. When I used the word we to refer to Aborigines, I did so not because I am Aboriginal, but because I had been asked to write on behalf of an Aboriginal organisation or group.

When I wrote the pamphlet The Stolen Generations in 1981, child separation was scarcely talked about. Non-Aborigines said that it couldn t have happened. The victims of separation thought it shameful, a shame job , to talk about their removal. They believed that maybe their parents had not been able to care for them properly, or worse still, didn t want them.

Eighteen years later, thousands of children throughout Australia have spoken out against the pain they endured, and are still enduring. So have the parents, and extended families of the children. Whole communities have expressed what it meant to have their families traumatised, their future leadership removed and blown to the four winds. Now we can see the policy for what it was—an attempt to terminate and prevent the reappearance of the nation's Indigenous people.

As the National Enquiry showed in 1995–96, the hurt of separation never ends. But at least now the non-Aborigines concede that the policy happened, and that it was wrong. The victims of separation understand that their families grieved for their children as much as the children grieved for them. State premiers and church leaders have apologised. There are now organisations carrying out Link-Up work in every state and the Northern Territory.

The last sentences of 'The Stolen Generations' were:

> Perhaps in time the whites will suffer in the knowledge of what they have done. But they cannot expect forgiveness.

Many readers in 1981 were upset by this conclusion. Now we can ask: Have they, after nearly twenty years, achieved forgiveness? My answer is No, they have not, despite the massive and thrilling wave of public sympathy before and during Sorry Day 1998. For the financial future of the Link-Up organisations is by no means, as yet, secure. There are not yet absolute legal guarantees that the separation process cannot begin again. And in August 1998 the Western Australian police, with government support, proposed to again begin separating certain Aboriginal children from their parents. Have we learnt nothing at all?

We must insist that Aboriginal children are never again separated from their families and those who are grieving be allowed to heal, whatever the cost. National reconciliation requires it, common humanity demands it.

Prologue

The Stolen Generations: Who are we?[1]

The 'Stolen Generations' have become an enormously powerful symbol (along with Mabo and Deaths in Custody) of the relationship between Aboriginal and non-Aboriginal Australia. Following the 1998 federal election Prime Minister Howard, evidently intending to promote reconciliation in his second term, could not see that an apology to the stolen generations was a prerequisite for that reconciliation. Shortly after the election he announced that 'It is not so much the fear of compensation claims that constrains me on that, it is a belief I have, a very genuine belief, that you express collective regret for things for which you are collectively and in a direct sense responsible . . . I don't think that applies to the current generation of Australians'.[2] Yet I will show in this book that every generation of Australians, including the current generation, for the last 210 years, is 'collectively and in a direct sense responsible' for what was done, by government and church, in the name of the Australian people.

So who are the Stolen Generations, what was done to them, and why does their fate haunt the Aboriginal community today? It would be easy to lose the individuals in the larger political nation, but throughout this book it is the individuals whom I have met and often worked with over the last 25 years that have been foremost in my mind. They include Joy Williams, baffled as to why she was taken from her mother and sent to a non-Aboriginal institution until she obtained the chilling committal notice—'Reason for admission: a fair skinned child to be taken from association with Aborigines'. Clarrie Nean, sent to jail for running away from the intolerable conditions of Kinchela, later found dead in a police cell. Russell Moore, adopted into a white family, later to commit a horrific murder in the US and to escape execution narrowly. And Jane King, doomed by psychological trauma endlessly and futilely to clean not only her flat, but the streets outside her home. While the stories are individual, each fragment fills out a picture of generations of separated children, one brush stroke at a time.

So who are the Stolen Generations? They may well say, with a single collective voice:

Why of course we are the children taken away from our families and put into the Aboriginal institutions, and who didn't return for years and years. Everyone knows that . . .

But we are also the children who were taken away who died in the institutions, or in mental hospitals, or in jail, or on the streets, and never came home at all.

We are the people who still do not know where our home is.

We are the mothers and fathers, aunties and uncles, grandmothers and grandfathers, cousins, brothers and sisters who never saw our children again.

We are the children who were sent to the non-Aboriginal institutions like Boystown and the Mittagong State Homes. We cannot even share the group memories of Moore River or Retta Dixon or Kinchela or Colebrook.

We are the children who were adopted and fostered who grew up thinking we were Indian, or Filipino, or Maori, or Indian.

We are the children who have spent our lives seeking acceptance in both the Aboriginal and the non-Aboriginal communities, and sometimes we have not found it in either.

We are the children and grandchildren of removed mothers and fathers who don't know which community or country we belong to.

We are the adopted children who are torn between the love of our adopting parents and our burning desire to go home to our old people.

We are the ones whose adoption broke down when we were teenagers and who have lived on the streets for years.

We are the old people who sit quietly in nursing homes. We are the toddlers who are growing up in suburban non-Aboriginal homes.

We are the ones who were taught to turn our backs on our own mother because she was too black.

We are the ones who have not even told our own children that we are Aboriginal.

We are the ones who will never come forward to tell our story because we are too ashamed.

We are unemployed, we are the coordinators of Aboriginal organisations, we lead national companies, we manage childcare agencies, we write books.

We live in Musgrave Park, we live in Charcoal Lane, we live in Vaucluse, we live in Fullerton, we live in Fannie Bay, we live in Sandy Bay.

What do we Stolen Generations have in common then? We Stolen Generations are the victims of Australia-wide policies which aimed to separate us from our parents, our family, our neighbourhood, our community, our country and our rightful inheritance as Aboriginal citizens of Australia. We are the victims of a policy which—if it had been success-ful—would have put an end to Aboriginality forever. Not just ours—everyone's. And we are still hurting.

1

The oral evidence

The first interview[1] I published with an Aboriginal person separated as a child was made with Veronica Cameron in 1976. Veronica Cameron lived near me in Katherine, Northern Territory and we often discussed her time as an institutionalised child at the Catholic children's home at Snake Bay, Melville Island. Veronica's account of the institution, like other narratives of the time, was ambiguous—neither resentful nor forgiving, accepting institutionalisation without blame, neither hating nor loving the nuns.

The parents of Topsy Nelson Napurrula were allowed to see their daughter a little more frequently, but the missionaries' equating traditional ways with 'rubbish' was little different from church teaching at Roper River 30 years before. She described her life at Phillip Creek, an Anglican institution near Tennant Creek, in the 1950s.

Topsy Nelson Napurrula related her escape from Phillip Creek with so much zest and hilarity that neither I, nor perhaps at this time Topsy Napurrula herself, understood how forced assimilation had collectively affected a whole people as well as thousands of individuals.

Two years later, in 1979, I was recording personal histories at Erambie Station, near Cowra, New South Wales, where, although I did not realise this at the time, some of the managers had used child removal to threaten and punish the station residents defying their arbitrary authority.

Aileen Wedge's life history, recorded at Erambie, is now recognisable to me as the first of the horror stories of institutionalisation and its consequences revealed in 'Bringing Them Home' eighteen years later. Yet at the time I spoke with her I still was not able to understand the tragedy of Aileen's life in anything but individual terms. Even her refusal to see her mother who had come to visit her at the Cootamundra Girls Home because she was 'too black' did not alert me to the catastrophically negative presentation of Aboriginality which she, and all the girls in the Cootamundra Home, were subjected to.

Joy Williams' story as well as any exemplifies the terrible long-term destruction which begins at the moment the children are apprehended by the state. There is Joy as bright as a button in the early photographs. At the age of twelve or thirteen she begins cutting her arms to find out what colour her blood is, and she grows up, she says, thinking she is stupid. Whatever else the state took from her, it could not extract her sharp natural intelligence. My friend Joy Williams, the accomplished poet, now holds a Master of Arts in Creative Writing.

All through the 1970s, I now realise, stories like those of Veronica, Topsy, Joy and Aileen had been accumulating, but we still saw only the individual tragedies, not the apocalypse.

'Oh what's this, cocky tucker?'
(*Veronica Cameron*)

Every morning (if you were on the cooking roster) you had to go and serve it out . . . Sometimes the older girls [i.e.

those working, not at school] used to have tinned meat. After breakfast there were dishes to wash, or scrub the refectory . . .

Then we'd go and do the washing, and hanging out the clothes. Then when that's finished Sister always had some other odd jobs to do, you couldn't sit down till about ten, that was smoko.

Then we'd go upstairs to do sewing, and if it was washing day for the nuns, we had to wash their big habits, and the brothers' trousers, and darn the socks, and the other girls did the ironing. And then one of the sisters used to show us how to starch—we didn't like that.

After lunch the Sisters used to have a bit of a rest, and then we'd do a job that needed doing, like over at the boys the pillow slips needed changing. We had no sheets, only blankets, so we only had to do the pillow slips. It depended on how the morning jobs went. The boys, up till 13, went to school, but later on there wasn't enough girls and boys for work, so they had to pull us out of school. I was about 13.

Meals were about 5. We had to hurry up because we had to go to the Rosary whether we liked to or not. The meals weren't very good, maybe a stew sometimes or open some tinned meat. sometimes for dessert there was just bread and milk in a big pot. 'Oh what's this—cocky tucker?' Sometimes there were big tins of fruit.

Recreation hour was from 7 till 8. There was a film sometimes or we did dances like the waltz, or the Dashing White Sergeant, or the girls did the twist.

'Don't go to that rubbish place'
(Topsy Nelson Napurrula)

Sometimes parents was come sometime, come and see us, and we was bit, bit, you know, we didn't sometimes, kids, we didn't much worry about mother and father now. We used to play one place, and stay one place because we was bit used to it.

[Q]: *You'd forget about your father and mother?*
Yeah

[Q]: *So, if there's a ceremony, or business on, you couldn't go?*
No.

[Q]: *What about during the day, Topsy? Did the mothers, the women, ever sing then so you sit with them?*
No, not in this place.

Because . . . because the missionary didn't allow much, can't see them business. The missionary was keep telling us:

'Ah, don't go that rubbish place [i.e. the ceremonial ground] and don't follow your mother and father. Gotta learn something. Gotta learn this way. Follow this one.'

[Q]: *You mean, follow Christian way?*
Yeah. Christian way. Whitefeller way. Whitefeller way . . .

[Q]: *Some kids run away from the mission?*
Yeah.

[Q]: *Where did they run to?*
Once I ask my mother and father they went away you know. And I went to camp and I ask one of them ladies, old ladies,

'Where's my mum and dad?'

And they said to me,

'They're gone'.

I came back, to dormitory. Afternoon time I was thinkin', and I couldn't stop cry. Just thinking for my mum, and cryin'.

Next day I got away.

[Q]: *Run away?*
Yuwayi [yes]

[Q]: *Which way'd you go?*
To Tennant Creek.

[Q]: *Did you walk?*

4

Yeah.

[Q]: *Your father and mother there? Did you find them?*

Yeah, yeah.

[Q]: *Which one did you go with?*

Nobody.

[Q]: *In the daytime, when you ran away?*

In night.

[Q]: *Night time! By yourself!*

And they was looking for me. And some other kids was telling them:

'Topsy's not here. She's gone. And she went, to be with
his [her] mother and father!'

Because my father took that other thing down to that
place, to that old Station, that old Telegraph Station, he
took goat there. And that's why I couldn't stay 'ere. So I was
keep thinking. And missionary was go down, and tryin' to
come and bring me back.

And I was run away again . . .

[Q]: *Some places, they lock those dormitories at night so the kids
can't get out?*

Yes, they used to do [that] here.

[Q]: *Did you get out through the window maybe?*

No, I was hiding. They was telling.

'Come on you kids, ready for bed!'

And I was creeping along.

I ended up at North Ryde
(*Joy Williams*)

[Q]: *What is your earliest memory?*

I remember when people used to come and visit us at
Bomaderry Home. There was a lady came with her lovely
silver belt buckle and it was Auntie Nuggo [Mrs Louisa

Ingram] and she always used to wear it with this blue flowery dress and I used to think she was my mother.

[I was at Bomaderry] till I was six. [Then] I went to Lutanda, that's a [Plymouth] Brethren Home. [At that time] it used to be in Wentworth Falls and I can still remember the train trip. I had a new tartan skirt and a red jumper and a blue coat and red patent leather shoes. I remember the steam train and one of the workers from Bomaderry took me to Lutanda. I remember we stopped at Strathfield because the station master, you know how you get the shrubs along the railway station, he had cut them into animal shapes. I remember an emu and a kangaroo. And I remember getting to Wentworth Falls 'cause I was given bread and milk, hot bread and milk, and it was raining and there was another little girl there and she was going to be the youngest. It's funny because I ended up in all the eighteen years, third eldest, so I went from second youngest to third eldest in 42 kids. And I was the only Koori [Aboriginal] kid there.

[Q]: *Were you ever told why you were there, instead of Cootamundra [Home specifically for Aboriginal girls]?*

No, I was never told of any decision even as I got older. But obviously there was a decision because a few years ago I wrote to the Home and asked why I was there and they sent me back a certificate that was made at Lutanda. I showed it to Mum, who'd signed it, but she told me it didn't have anything written on it when she signed it, and that was '47. It says 'Reason for admission: a fair skinned child to be taken from association with Aborigines'.

[Q]: *What was it like at Lutanda?*

Well I've been told I should be grateful. Very difficult! Very straight, very religious. I think I was converted six million times—was saved. That entailed another piece of cake on Sunday. Had nice clothes, always had plenty of food. There was always a big changeover of staff so there wasn't any use getting attached to anyone. [After the Home moved to Sydney] I went to Hornsby Girls High, was told I should be grateful for that.

[Q]: *When did you learn that you were Koori?*

When I was about eleven. I wondered why I didn't have any visitors. They had visiting days, the first Saturday of every month, and I used to wait at the top of the gate for Mum. See, at Christmas I was the only kid left in the Home, and they used to sorta draw lots to see who was going to take me home with them, otherwise somebody'd have to stay at the Home to look after me. Practically drew lots. But I wasn't happy with that, that's when I started running away. I spent the night—nothing happened though—with this fellow at Hornsby. Next thing they hauled me down to the cop shop at Hornsby, and that's where they told me. I was given an internal, and I was still a virgin, much to their surprise. And when I got back to the Home, I got a hiding with a butter-pat, and I had to write 500 times 'God is love'.

The only Koori I'd ever heard of was Albert Namatjira. Look at the cuts on me arms. I started doing that when I was about twelve, 'cause I wanted to find out what colour me blood was. Nobody wanted me there—only to work. I was looking after the girls all the time when I was sixteen. I grew up thinking I was ugly and stupid. I didn't think anyone wanted me. I used to watch those girls being fostered out: nobody wanted me. Angry most of the time. Always attention-seeking, whether it was good or bad. That's why I was converted so many times, they were all over you like a rash.

Then they put me in the Nurses' Home at Parramatta District. The majority of [Lutanda] girls went to business college in Hornsby, I went to the nurses' quarters. The first thing I did was to get a picture of the Everly Brothers and stick it on with nail polish on me mirror, 'cause we were never allowed to do those sort of things [at Lutanda]. They were heathen! And I used to sneak in and put the wireless on, real soft, and hear 'Diana' and then I'd have it on ABC and I'd hear Harold Blair, that was nice too, John McCormack. That's where I got used to Beethoven.

[Q]: How long were you nursing?

Not long! I remember my roster was such that I started off with two days off, so I went back to Lutanda. All the girls went home on their days off, so I went. And they said, 'No, Joy, you can't come back here, you live at the nurses' quarters now, that's where you have to stay'. I was sixteen, just over. I was put into male surgical, doing dirty pans and trotting round with bottles, a nursing aide more, I think. But I ended up at North Ryde [mental hospital] as a patient. I had a little six months in jail, on remand, and I was offered either to go to North Ryde Psychiatric or a conviction, and I was cunning enough to take North Ryde.

[Q]: What happened at North Ryde?

We were put in pyjamas for seven days, then they worked out our medication. Had to go down to groups twice a day, I think, and they just tried different things like Stellazine, Melsaden, Tryptanol, Tofranil, Largactil—good old Largactil— Mogadon and barbiturates. See when I started nursing one of the senior nurses gave me some amphetamines to keep me awake. I asked her what it was and she said Methedrine and I liked the feel of that. Then I was getting sleeping tablets at night, Phenobarb or something like that. Carbital. Junkie! In groups you're supposed to talk about your innermost feelings, and I know it now as confrontation therapy. If you said you felt good, everybody'd be on to you till you felt absolutely rotten, so you weren't allowed to say how you really felt, because you'd end up feeling exactly the reverse. I got pretty clever at that, pretty cluey, and in the small groups we'd turn it round and just practise it on one of the nurses or something.

Then you were allowed weekend leave, and I used to choof down to the city, and that's where I met the fellow I married. Had me baby at North Ryde. I took off again, and when I came back they got a male nurse to take me over to St. Anthony's [Catholic Home, Croydon] with my daughter and I didn't sign anything then. I'm *told* I signed adoption papers, but I was very heavily sedated at the time. I used to be on 600 mls of Largactil a day, then Stellazine and bloody Melsadon at night. Should've killed an elephant. I took off and didn't go back. Haven't been back since.

'I'd never put anybody in jail'
(Aileen Wedge)

Mummy used to go to Sydney every year. She had three holes in her hip, and it used to leak all the time, and she had to go to Sydney all the time to get it treated. She was crippled like that since she was a girl. Aggie [Agnes Coe] cared for us then, they were living up there in that first house. Then I got sent to the nuns' home. But they chucked me out of that. They cut my long hair off. I didn't like it, so I ripped their clothes off the line. A lot of girls had their hair cut short, but my mummy, she told them not to cut my hair, but they cut it. So I started cutting their clothes up. I was only there for a couple of months. They sent me off to La Perouse then, stayed there a couple of weeks, then they brought me home.

Aggie had Archie [the next eldest brother] and Callaghan [Paul Coe snr] had had Colin [another brother]. He [Colin] was always buttin' in, so that was that. When my mother came home from hospital, he said the kids are not staying with no one, they're going back to the home. He said

9

don't send Aileen back to the nuns' home 'cause they treat all the black girls down there [badly], make 'em do all the hard work. Best place to send her is over to Cootamundra 'cause it's an Aborigine home for girls. Better off over there, and Archie would be better off at Kinchela 'cause there's all the dark boys up there. And Colin went to Boystown. So he went and seen the manager.

[Q]: *Did you have to work at Cootamundra?*

If you wanted to go to the pictures, matinees, you had to go and do gardening. That's for the pocket-money. Like, we used to get an allowance from the government. It used to go into a banking account for us, when we got out. But most of the girls, when they turned sixteen, they'd give them a live-in job. All the women over there were white people, except the cook. She was a black woman, Miss Barlow.

[Q]: *Did they treat you all right?*

Not me, I was muckin' up all the time. I used to go and pinch the eggs, and get the fowls, and kill 'em, and chuck 'em in the incinerator and eat 'em when they're cooked. I didn't like it over there. When I got presents from me father I had to share them with all, you know. I was made to share them. And if you started fighting, the police would come and take you and put you in the jail for the night.

Right on top of a big hill it is. Big garden all around. You can go out in the garden and you can see all Cootamundra. Nice old place, if it was done up nice. It was an old hospital, and they had a box-room—they used to *call* it the box-room—I think it was a morgue, where they used to put the people that died. When you used to muck up, they used to lock the door. The slide thing used to be there. When you used to muck up, they used to lock you in that, and put the lights out, and make it real dark in there, real cold.

[Q]: *Were you put in there often?*

I used to live in there. One woman over there, she used to
hit the big girls, and they [she] ended up breaking a girl's
back with a brick. Her name was Mrs Prosser [fictitious
name]. She got hit by her, with a brick, in her back. Broke
her back, and they ended up sacking her. But I only got
locked in the box-room. I used to fight with the other girls.
Some of us, we shot through one night, about eighteen of us.
When they caught us they put us in jail for the night. Then
on Sundays we'd go to church in town if we wanted to, but
they usually had a service at night time. Woman there she
used to play the piano, we'd all sing hymns by that.
[Q]: *Why were you so against the rules, do you think?*
I dunno, just the way I was, I guess. Mischievous.
[Q]: *Did you get many visitors?*
No. My father, he always used to come over on pension day,
Christmas day, and me birthday. When I was in mental hospitals, and down in Parramatta [girl's reformatory], he used to
be always there, to visit me. I think I missed him more than
I missed me mother I reckon. One day a lot of Erambie
people came to see me. I was frightened. They looked different from the other blacks that was with me. I wouldn't even
go out to me mother. I said, 'No, she's too black,' and she
was whiter than some of the girls over there.
[Q]: *How did you find the local High School?*
I got chucked out of High School. That's when they sent me
home. Chucked a pot of stew over a teacher. That's when
they sent me home then, said I could go to school here. At
school there, I used to walk out of class and go down the
street all the time, that's why the matron got sick of it.
    . . . I'm a dunce now. I don't know nothing. I can read.
I can't spell, but I can read. I started taking tablets then,
drinking fly spray and everything like that.
[Q]: *Were you unhappy at home, do you think?*
Well I didn't really know my mother, you know what I

mean? I wasn't with her much. My father was with me all
the time. Anyway, Haines got me sent away from Erambie as
'uncontrollable'. So I got sent to Parramatta Girls Home and
from there to North Ryde. And from there I lost count of all
the other places.

It was worse at Parramatta. Girls were crueller, and the
men used to look after 'em. They had women there too, but
the men were the heads. But the other girls were cruel, used
to just punch you. But most of the homes you go to, or gaol,
they don't seem to pick on the blacks. Just the white people
seem to get most of the things, get hurt and that. Even in
Long Bay Jail, none of the blacks used to get hurt there.
They stick together. If one gets hit, they've got to fight the
lot. But I never used to muck up there, 'cause if I did, they'd
send me to a mental hospital.

[Q]: What for?

Nerves I suppose. And mum used to reckon I was stupid,
guangi. That's how I was born. I started to cut myself all the
time. Me face, me legs, me body. Put berries in me ears.
They sent me to Ryde, and then Darlinghurst, and then
Callan Park, and then Glebe, and then over to Orange, then
North Ryde, all mental hospitals about seven or eight times.

When I used to go to Orange over here, Doc always
wanted to put me in voluntary so I could come out when I
wanted to. They wanted to give me shock treatment, but
Doc wouldn't let them. Old [Dr] Bill McClaren here, he told
them not to do it on me. I was signed in, see. If I was sen-
tenced in by a court, then they could do it on me. I was
signed in, see. That time I tried to push a nurse off a second-
floor building up here, well the police wanted to sign me in,
take me to court for it, but old Bill said, 'No, she goes in voluntary.' I've seen some of them get it. They put 'em to sleep,
and they put a plug in their mouth, and get hold of the lips
like that. They got two, like, iron things. Put this big

machine on, high noise, and they put two of them [wires] together like that. And they KICK! like that, when the electricity is goin' through you. Most of the people over there that I seen get it done, was people they call split personality. It didn't seem to help them at all. They're still stupid. But I just had medicine. Just kept me drugged-up. Not over at Orange, only down at North Ryde. And now my son Colin, the one I had over in Orange—I had a baby in the mental hospital—my mother had him taken off me.

[Q]: *How old was he?*

Couple of months. He wouldn't even be two months. I had him in the base hospital. I was there for twelve days, they sent me home. Had him for about a month, I think, and mummy went and seen old Bill McClaren, and I had to go to court. I wasn't classed fit enough to have him. That's me own mother's doing. They asked her in court, would she take him. And she said, 'You can see I'm crippled. I can't take a young baby.'

He was made a ward of the state.

[Q]: *Did they ask your opinion?*

I couldn't. I wasn't allowed to say about the kid, 'cause they knew I had him in the mental hospital.

[Q]: *Do you think you were looking after him all right?*

Yeah. But my mother was frightened, see. She was frightened I might hurt him.

[Q]: *Do you think you would have?*

I don't know. I was real sick then. He'd be fifteen now. When he was about nine, I went down to Sydney, and they brought him down to the children's welfare place in King Street. See, the people that had him, they took him when he went to the homes. He was fostered over to them and I was told I had no chance of getting him back unless I was married. So they sent me a letter to come to the child welfare place, and they said I could see him on one condition: would

13

I sign the papers over to the people that had him. So they
could adopt him. Well the woman that's got him, she was a
black gin [Aboriginal woman]—she couldn't have no kids. So
she's got him. Lives at Crows Nest.

[Q]: *Would you want to see him again?*

No. See him again and I'd want to take him then. He'll probably come home. They always do. That was the first time
he'd seen me. But didn't call me missus or anything, he just
called me mum. He's still in my name.

[Q]: *Could you tell me about your time in Long Bay?*

That was for assaulting, grievous bodily harm. I assaulted
Tiny. Mummy was there and Shirley and Flo. They was all
fighting who was going to bash Tiny up. Mummy was bash-
ing her with the crutch. It was terrible—I couldn't even get
a punch in. Mummy wouldn't let me have a go. She wanted
to have a go. But I walked into the house first, see, and I
punched her through the window, she was cheeking me
through the window. Smashed the glass and the glass cut her.
We all go outside, and the police come then. I already had a
fine on me. So I had a couple of months at Long Bay. It was
better in the jail than at the home. You had to work, but
they weren't so strict like at Parramatta. Get plenty of good
food there, plenty to eat. Only thing I didn't like was night-
time when they lock you in the cell. I was on an easy job. I
used to go round and collect the garbage, go out near the
gate, go up to where a screw used to live, go round all the
rooms and pick up the rubbish. I was finished then. I just
used to muck around, and go and help them in the kitchen.

Parramatta was terrible. There's too many lesbians there.
Used to make me sick. That's why I started putting needles
in me legs, to get out of it. And if a girl liked you, they used
to get jealous of you, fight over you. God, they were terrible.
There was one man there, he was the second head bloke, he
used to ask the girls to see him. If they said no he used to

14

bash them. But they found out about him and he got sacked. But there was never a black gin he'd ask, always the white girls.

They had a little jail there. If you'd muck up, they'd lock you in the little jail. One blanket chucked in with you. Sleep on the cement floor. I wouldn't like to be in the jail they put you in when you muck up at Long Bay. It's just real dark in there it is, and you can't go to the toilet, they don't give you nothing to use or anything. I've never been in it, but I've seen inside it.

[Q]: *Was it harder because you were black?*

No. In jail, or at Parramatta, the blacks would stick together. One got hit, they had to fight the lot. They'd all be in there, a little group by themselves all the time. And the women screws, they never used to muck around with the blacks, give 'em a rough go, 'cause they used to behave themselves.

[Q]: *Are you angry with your mother and father now?*

No, she couldn't look after us. She used to go in at the beginning of the year, and come out at the end. All the time like that.

[Q]: *Do you think it would have been hard for her to have had her last three kids taken away?*

Oh yeah, I suppose so, but who got hurt the most, when we got sent away? Sidney, me father, 'cause I was his favourite. It didn't matter where I was, he was always there to see me. He wasn't actually worried about me brothers, just me.

[Q]: *What was the worst of all the places you've been in?*

Callan Park. North Ryde was open, real poshy people used to be there. Have your own room. People getting married there and everything. Callan Park—that's wicked. They're real mental there, real *guangi*. I was always sleeping. Always had some split personalities. Some used to do silly things. One old woman over there, she used to eat spiders.

[Q]: You don't cut yourself any more?
No, not since Benny my husband died. He was cruel. He hit me on the head with the axe, broke me ribs. He split me head open. Another inch and they said me brains would have popped out.
[Q]: Did you ever think of putting him in?
Never ever. I'd never put anybody in jail.

2

The written evidence

In the very first year of the colony of New South Wales, in acts that were to symbolise what followed, Arthur Phillip ordered the capture and imprisonment of two Aboriginal people. His motives were complex, but among them was the hope that if these men could be kept separate from their 'primitive' society they could be educated and civilised and act as emissaries to black society to bring about its change. For 210 years, Aboriginal children have continued to be removed, in astonishingly large numbers, for similar reasons. This chapter looks at the history of the process.

Why separate Aboriginal children?[1]

Non-Aborigines traditionally have subdivided the Indigenous people of Australia into categories of their own devising, such as traditional/non-traditional, 'full blood'/'half-caste', urban/rural, north/south. The separation of Aboriginal children has been justified by mentally labelling them as 'needing to be separated from their communities', though which children precisely were in that category varied from one period to another.

Those categories most relevant here, always much more obvious to those who did the dividing than to those being divided, were the apparent dichotomies of child/parent and full Aboriginal descent/part-descent.

Child/parent

In the early years of the colonies, when there were very few children of part-Aboriginal descent, the whites seized upon the children as potentially different from their parents. Missionaries believed, and wanted to demonstrate to the other whites, that Aboriginal children were made in God's image and educable to the level of white domestic servants and labourers. Most of the separations carried out in the early decades of the colonies were made on the supposition that children represented innocence and hope while, the adults represented reaction and superstition.

The missionaries at the Wellington Valley mission in New South Wales in the 1830s were preoccupied by this distinction between parent and child. One of them, William Watson, was a single minded obsessive intent on gathering as many children together as he could. His associate, the Reverend James Gunther, preferred indoctrination to force. He taught his class of pre-initiated Aboriginal boys that their elders were 'wicked old fellows' and recorded this conversation in his diary:

> Cochrane: [one of the boys] I must go to the camp, the old men make me go.
> Gunther: What need you these wicked old fellows?
> Cochrane: Why care you for the Governor? These old men our Governors, we must do what they say.

18

Nineteenth century missionaries had no answer to such logic other than force, though to be fair to Gunther, not all were prepared to kidnap their young charges. Watson was.

Late in 1838 Watson quit the Wellington Valley mission altogether to set up a second, unofficial mission at the site of the present Aboriginal reserve. There he kept prisoner and instructed the little children. Throughout 1939 Gunther heard disturbing rumours of Watson's high-handed methods of removing children from their parents. Then on 16 December 1839 there occurred an archetypal but chilling event which marked a turning point in the missionaries' relations with the Wiradjuri: and White Australia with Aboriginal Australia.

In the hot mid-afternoon of 16 December 1839 Watson went down to the riverside camp of the Wiradjuri people to remove a two year old child from her mother Poll Plunkett, who, so he claimed, had sold her to him for eleven pounds. Poll refused. Her relatives rushed to her aid as Watson tried to snatch the child. Pandemonium ensued as Watson struck out at everyone within reach. Quick as a flash, one of her relatives grabbed the screaming child and made off with her to Gunther's house for protection. There he thrust her into the arms of Gunther's Aboriginal maid, Poll Buckley. Poll Buckley retreated inside while Watson, unable to get in, went for the constables and presently arrived at a run. Scarlet with anger, he demanded that the child, whose screams could clearly be heard from the Gunthers' bedroom, be handed to him. Gunther refused. 'A fine thing', stormed Watson, 'a Christian missionary being opposed by his fellow labourer'. His features [according to Gunther in his diary] grew 'quite disturbed', his mind 'hardly able to hear a word of reasoning'. After several minutes Watson pushed his way past the defenders, forced his way inside, seized the child and decamped with her to his station. The uproar was profound. Gunther recorded in his diary that Polly Plunkett, and all the women present, were 'screaming bitterly'. Well might Gunther reflect that night that this 'disgraceful stain' on the missionaries' character was 'very unfortunate' for their work. Watson henceforth was known as 'the eaglehawk' and relations between the missionaries and the blacks were soured for good.

Two weeks later, because there was not a single person on the mission to instruct, Gunther went on a journey through the bush. In the course of a week he found many of his boys at various camps and stations—at least he knew now where they got to when they left him. More disturbing was that he found most of the women and all of the children had put themselves out of reach before he arrived. Some he could see watching him from the other side of the river, others peered down at him from the tops of trees. Gunther's fears were confirmed. The Wiradjuri had heard that the *parton* (the Wiradjuri language has no 'rs' sound) was coming and assumed it was Watson coming for the kids. That fear of abrupt and arbitrary child-removal was to dwell with Aboriginal Australians for the next 160 years.

Part-descent/ full-descent

Probably the part-Aboriginal population, that is, the people of part-white/Aboriginal descent who lived with and identified as Aborigines, began to increase in New South Wales after 1850, but because the whites were not yet well established in the rural districts, little attention was drawn to the fact. It was not till the 1880s that those individuals who were self-confident enough to complain to the New South Wales government, such as newspaper editors and bankers, began to draw attention to the Aboriginal populations gathering round their towns. They demanded that the authorities take measures to control what had rapidly become, to them, an increasing rather than a decreasing problem: that though the numbers of 'full blood' Aborigines were diminishing, those of part-descent were not only increasing but gathering down by the river in what they called 'the blacks camp'.

So a century after the invasion, separations were justified on a second distinction drawn by the categorisers between 'full blood' and 'half-caste' Aborigines. The distinction was quite artificial; for example, it is likely that in 1900, most Aboriginal children in southern Australia had two self-identifying, reserve dwelling, Aboriginal parents, some of whom may indeed have been of part-white descent, but the only point that mattered was that the parents lived together as Aborigines on the reserve or camp. Other Aborigines and the people themselves, (as well as the whites who lived nearby) thought of them as Aboriginal.

Through genetic chance, some of the children in any family were likely to be lighter coloured than others. In a family of six children of two part-Aboriginal parents, it was and is common for skin colouring to range between very dark to quite fair, with maybe a red-head as well. Yet despite the identical parentage, the lighter children were likely to be treated by state and church officials as if they were potentially different in character from their own brothers and sisters of darker colouring. Aboriginal identification, by contrast, was by association and a shared culture and belief system, as well as the exercise of obvious rule of thumb genetics: 'I'm your mother and I'm Aboriginal so you're an Aboriginal too'. The difference between the ways in which the Indigenous and non-Indigenous identified Aboriginality was complicated by the white assumption that the part-European genetic inheritance, interpreted crudely by lighter skin colouring, allowed the programming of an individual for life amongst the Europeans. At base, however, the 'half-caste' distinction was convenient. It was political. In the Northern Territory, part-

Aboriginal children were institutionalised in large numbers because the government feared that otherwise they would swamp the small white population.[2] Even in the south, where the disproportion of whites to Aborigines was huge, the fear remained that the state might be threatened by the uprising of a 'wild race of half-castes'.[3]

Although we can see parallels between separating Aboriginal children and removing children from industrial slums in Britain, the added colonial characteristic seems to be the hatred and contempt for Aboriginal people. The origins of this hatred lie deep-rooted in guilt over the invasion. How much more convenient it would have been for the whites had the Aborigines disappeared completely as for a time it seemed they would do in southern Australia.

We can now pinpoint some motives for separation, both political and convenient. Underlying the authorities' endless divisions of 'half-caste', 'quadroon' and 'octoroon' was the principle that, in the long term, Aborigines were not wanted—anywhere. Their extinction, it seemed, would not occur naturally after all, but would have to be arranged. It is in this way that we should interpret the ironically named Aboriginal Protection Acts which were passed by all the mainland state governments by 1912 (for example, Western Australia 1905, South Australia 1911) which allowed for the permanent removal of children. Their mainspring was that the Aboriginal population had increased, was increasing and ought to be diminished. The removal and institutionalisation of the children was to be a principal weapon of the new Acts.

Inefficiency, lack of funds and lack of state support had so far prevented large numbers of Aboriginal children being removed. Whatever the effect on the Aboriginal families of the nineteenth century, disease, killings and dispossession were the prime disasters for their civilisation, not enforced separations.

Massive intervention by the state in the lives of Aboriginal families became the central catastrophe only in twentieth-century Aboriginal Australia. The nineteenth-century desire to 'save' the children was now overlain by a much more pragmatic and sinister intention to scatter Indigenous children throughout white institutions and homes. The desire to prevent the children from becoming 'a positive menace to the state', as the NSW Aborigines Protection Board put it, was coupled neatly with the theory that separated and 'trained' Aboriginal children would become a positive asset. The Secretary of the South Australian State Children's Council told a 1913 Royal Commission:

> I am . . . strongly of the opinion that if we took these native children when they were quite infants . . . we could educate them for service . . . and they would do useful work for the community. . . . They should be taken away directly they are born. If they are in the wurley [bark shelter] for a week it is bad for them, but it is fatal for them to remain there a year.[4]

By 1950, when removals were probably at their peak (one in three or four children in New South Wales), all states and territories except Tasmania possessed a number of well-known, and now notorious, institutions of church and state in which children were incarcerated. They included Carrolup, Roeburn, Mt Margaret, Moore River (Western Australia), Colebrook (South Australia) Cherbourg, Palm Island and Woorabinda (Queensland), Kahlin and The Bungalow (Northern Territory) and Kinchela and Cootamundra (New South Wales).[5] Some of these institutions, such as the infamous Moore River settlement in Western Australia, were for adults and children combined, while others were just for children. Terrible deeds occurred at every one of them. One fifteen-year-old girl was imprisoned in a tiny cell at Moore

River for 67 days during 1918–19 for repeatedly attempting to run away to rejoin her family living off the reserve.[6]

The combined institutions kept adults and children apart by a few hundred metres just as effectively as the all-children institutions did by hundreds of kilometres. Hagar Roberts, of the Anglican Roper River Mission in the Northern Territory, recalled:

> Missionary didn't let us go, you see. She bin learn us to speak, like, white man way. Know about a white God story, teaching us to know what to do longa white man way, that story. They didn't let us go to mother and father.[7]

Critics of the policy of 'separation-by-dispersal' have been vocal at all periods of our history. Governments countered with 'separation-for-their-own-good'. In 1911 the NSW Aborigines Protection Board claimed that:

> the only chance these children have is to be taken away from their present environment and properly trained by earnest workers before being apprenticed out, and having once left the aborigines' reserves they should never be allowed to return to them permanently.[8]

Let's not forget the parents. In the last decade the focus of the media, which suddenly 'discovered' the stories of removed children, has been the experiences of children rather than their parents. The close families of separated children have also, of course, suffered greatly. Parents rarely completely recover from the shock of separation. Either as a Link-Up case worker or as a historian I have worked with many mothers who suffered appalling experience. They suffered agonies in not knowing the whereabouts of their children, or by watching their progress, by proxy, in photographs in the authorities' magazines! One mother whose child was to be adopted had a blanket thrown over her in childbirth so she could not catch a glimpse of her child. A far-western New South Wales woman whose child was forcibly removed saw her baby's photograph in the paper a month later under the heading 'Wanted for Adoption'. A Cowra woman whose child was removed at birth was told, when he was eleven, that she could meet him just once provided she signed an adoption consent form. Another mother was told by the same authority which owned the house she lived in, that, unless she left the reserve, her children would be removed because they were living in an unsatisfactory dwelling! Parents were threatened with charges of carnal knowledge, negligence or vagrancy unless they committed their children. Then their children vanished, often forever. Bob Randall, another removed person, put the anguish of his own and every other mother into his song, 'Brown Skin Baby'.

> As a young black preacher I used to ride
> My quiet pony round the countryside
> In a native camp I'll never forget
> A young black mother her cheeks all wet
>   Yowie!
>   My brown skin baby they take him away
> . . .
> The child grew up and had to go
> From the mission home that he loved so
> To find his mother he tried in vain
> Upon this earth they never met again.
>   Yowie!
> My brown skin baby they take him away.[9]

How many children?

It is impossible to quantify the total number of separations for several reasons. One is that some state governments have been reluctant to release the information regarding the number of children formally removed under child welfare legislation; another is that more detailed research is needed in states such as Victoria, where the records of children in the many church homes were not centralised; thirdly, an unknown number of children were removed illegally, for whom records naturally do not exist.

My estimation of 100,000 'separations' in *The Lost Children* in 1988 has been misunderstood. That's far too high; the actual figure is closer to 50,000. The 100,000 actually referred to Australian citizens who, I estimated, at that time did not then identify as Aborigines but *who were entitled to do so because their parent or grandparent had been removed*.[10] The consequences of non-identification by descendants of removed people, due to their lack of knowledge or shame in admitting the fact, have been much underestimated even by the Human Rights Commission Enquiry into the separation policy.

Consider this model scenario: An Aboriginal woman of fair complexion is removed from her family as a toddler. At an institution she is subjected to the denigration of her Aboriginality both as a concept and as represented by herself. At fourteen she leaves the dormitory for a rural property to become a maid, or 'house girl'. Here she remains for six or seven years. She is much too ashamed and frightened to return to her own home and family, of whose identity and whereabouts she is in any case uncertain. At 22 she marries a white man to whom she bears four children. Her own Aboriginality is a closed secret between her and her husband; only one or two neighbours even suspect. Naturally she raises her children as white, and the family represents, at this point, a loss to the Aboriginal race of five individuals including herself. Suppose now that her four children have four children each: now in three generations 21 Aborigines have been lost.

While absolute numbers are currently impossible to reckon, the potential for state governments to reduce drastically the number of identifying Aborigines within three or four decades can be seen to be enormous.

New South Wales, for example

In 1982 I estimated that 5625 children had been removed from their families between 1883 and 1969.[11] That figure now appears to have been an underestimation. A surer figure can be estimated on the approximately 84,000 files held by the NSW Welfare Service of all children in care in the period 1921, when records began, to 1985.[12] If 15 per cent of the children represented in these files were Aboriginal, (which is possibly an underestimation) the number of New South Wales children would therefore be close to 10,000. This figure is the number of removed children, not their descendants. The total number of New South Wales individuals deprived of an Aboriginal identity, as reasoned above, would be much higher than this.

The process of child removal began in New South Wales and probably proportionally affected more Aboriginal people than anywhere else. It is worth looking at the state in more detail.

To 1850, by which time all the initial New South Wales Christian missions had failed, perhaps not more than 400 Aboriginal children had been institutionalised. Between 1883 (when the Aborigines Protection Board was established) and 1900, several more hundred New South Wales children had been removed from their parents for one reason or another by missionaries, educators and state officials.

The turning point that divides the first hundred years of white settlement in New South Wales from the second, and the mostly Christian-inspired separations from the mostly strategic, was the question of whether an individual of part-descent was to identify as white or black. Many, however, remained. The relevant Act which applied to all children, the *Neglected Children and Juvenile Offenders Act*, allowed magistrates to place a child in the care of its extended family; sometimes they refused to commit children who were demonstrably well cared for. In 1980 I met an elderly woman in Narrandera who told me how, as a child of ten, she had been brought before the district magistrate as a neglected child. The Board wanted to place her in the dormitory of the Warangesda mission. The magistrate ruled that the girl appeared well fed and well cared for, ordering merely that her parents move close enough to the town to allow her to attend school.

The Aborigines Protection Board was not satisfied with this apparently defective mechanism whereby a magistrate could escape his responsibilities! It wanted greater statutory power to control the growing Aboriginal adult and child populations, and began lobbying members of parliament to enact specific legislation for the purpose. The result was the New South Wales *Aborigines Protection Act 1909*, which empowered the Aborigines Protection Board to 'assume full control and custody of the child of any aborigine, if after due enquiry it is satisfied that such a course is in the interest of the moral and physical welfare of such child'.[13] The absolute control granted to Station Managers or Inspectors in relation to children was echoed in the wide ranging powers available to the Board generally, which included expulsion of individuals or families from an Aboriginal reserve, and the revocation of existing reserves. From 1909 until the 1950s the policy of the removal of children remained a principal arm of the Board's stated aim of 'solving the Aboriginal problem forever'.

Nevertheless the new Act still provided for voluntary

rather than compulsory mass-separations. The *Neglected Children and Juvenile Offenders Act*, still adjudicated by magistrates rather than Board officials, remained the relevant law in matters of clear neglect or delinquency. Since separations per se, rather than welfare of possibly neglected children, was the Board's chief preoccupation, the *Aborigines Protection Act 1909* was held to be too weak not long after its enactment, and the officials again began plotting an amendment which would make long-term removals to institutions (not to other families) compulsory.

In 1915 the Act was amended. The government's purpose, as its representative stated in the New South Wales Parliament, was to 'break up the Aboriginal camps entirely'.[14] A magistrate would no longer be required. Under the amendment, the removal of children could now take place when the Board, after due enquiry, was 'satisfied that such a course was in the moral and physical welfare of the child'.[15] The state had voted itself almost unlimited powers to control Aborigines' present and future. By the end of the First World War it possessed the authority to remove from its reserves, whether managed or not, all children under eighteen years, and (under a 1918 amendment) men who in the opinion of the Board should have been earning a living elsewhere; and all people of more than half European descent (whatever that meant). Many families now left the reserves in order to better protect their children from the officials. In 1924 the government established the second of its two institutions specifically to re-educate and re-socialise Aboriginal children. The Kinchela home for boys was to achieve a notoriety even greater than that of the girls home at Cootamundra.

The wider context of child removal is again revealed not as misguided missionary or bureaucratic zeal but a concerted effort by the state to terminate and further prevent Aboriginal self-identification. That was exactly what happened to Joy

Williams, who described her experiences in Chapter 1: she was to be removed 'from association of aborigines as she [was] a fair-skinned child'. It was simple, and as cruel and as callous, as that. The government did not disguise its fundamental policy of dispersing the adults and separating the children, and the policy was further enforced during the following decades. Though the law regarding children was by 1918 so wide as to need no further amendment, in 1936 the *Aborigines Protection Act* was amended so that a magistrate could order an Aborigine from a fringe camp if he or she was found to be living in 'undesirable conditions'. An 'Aborigine' (technically a 'full blood or half-caste native') was only, however, 'Aboriginal' when described as such by the arresting officer. By definition, any fringe camp was undesirable to a policeman. Since it was then up to the accused to prove that he or she was not Aboriginal, it followed that the state had acquired the remarkable power to arrest any person on suspicion of being Aboriginal and remove him or her from that fringe camp.

Dragging a man away to jail for living with his extended family was no more than a microcosm of the policy agreed upon in a national conference in 1937. This was the future of Aborigines as set out by a conference of state and Commonwealth Aboriginal administrators:

> The destiny of the natives of Aboriginal origin, but not of the full descent, lies in their ultimate absorption by the people of the Commonwealth.[16]

In 1940 the NSW government, in keeping with the new policy, added 'the assimilation of Aborigines' to the purposes which the NSW Board was to pursue.[17]

The Board was abolished in 1969, leaving over a thousand children in institutional or family care. Almost none of them was being raised by Aboriginal adults, still less by their own extended families. The New South Wales child welfare system retained its hostility towards this form of care until the *Children (Care and Protection) Act 1987*, which provided the first placement preference as the child's own extended family, followed by placement in its own community, then within another Aboriginal family, and lastly in an Aboriginal institution or family which the Director-General of Welfare may choose after consultation with the child's family.[18]

Wiradjuri country, for example

Wiradjuri country is the south-central area of New South Wales and is one of the largest groupings of related families in the state. It received the particular attention of the Board's welfare officers because up to 1924 it contained two of the state's major managed reserves, and because up to 1969 it contained one of the few remaining managed Aboriginal stations, Erambie (Cowra). Erambie was regarded as one of the administration's toughest problems.

Two of these earliest managed Board stations were Warangesda, near Darlington Point, and Brungle, near Tumut. Warangesda was the earliest mission station to be created following the state's revived interest in 'protecting' its Aborigines (1879), and it was to Warangesda that children were sent in increasing numbers from 1893, when the government assumed control of the station from the missionaries. Until the establishment of the Cootamundra Girls Home in 1911, the Warangesda 'dormitory' became one of only two institutions in the state which received the young girls whom the Board had managed to entice or forcibly remove from their parents. Naturally these children included large numbers from surrounding Wiradjuri country.

Possibly some one hundred Wiradjuri children were removed and placed in Warangesda between the time of the establishment of the Board in 1883 and the *Aborigines Protection Act* in 1909. One such separated child was Paul Coe, who was charged with being neglected under the *Neglected Children and Juvenile Offenders Act* in 1911 and sent to the state institution at Mittagong. He recalled how as he grew older he had to escort the boys leaving the institution for farming jobs to the station to catch the train. He had to tell them that they were going home to stop them running away.[19]

The Board did not manage to catch all the children it wanted. Mrs Isobel Edwards told the story how, shortly before Warangesda was closed in 1924, her father saved her from the clutches of the Child Welfare Inspector:

> Well next day [Inspector] Donaldson came to our home and he asked mum if she had the children ready, and she said 'No, and you're not taking them'. Then dad stepped out from the bedroom door with a double-barrelled shotgun he had and he said 'you lay your hands on my kids Donaldson and you'll get this'. Donaldson said 'Put that gun away Murray, put the gun away'. And dad said 'You touch those kids and your brains will splatter . . . the roof.' I know it's not a nice thing to say, but he had to frighten him somehow. Anyway, when old dad stepped towards him old Donaldson went for his life.[20]

Better personal and statistical records exist of the Wiradjuri children removed after 1945. Perhaps another 40 children were removed in the period 1945–67 for a range of offences including the theft of two empty soft drink bottles, for which two Cowra boys were sent to the corrective 'Borstal' at Mt Penang. It is clear that, despite a contrary instruction in the Manager's Handbook, officials used to threaten parents with removing their children if, say, their houses were untidy. Flo Doolan, of Erambie Station, remembered:

> The boys got sent to Kempsey [Kinchela] I think it was,

and the girls got sent to Cootamundra. Auntie Shirley went off at [the Manager], had a row and he summonsed Auntie Shirley. Auntie Shirley beat him in court for whatever it was, and to get back at her, well he got them sent away for being neglected.[21]

Such memories are verified when we know more about Cowra itself. Cowra Aborigines at this time were particularly victimised by the authorities of Health Inspector, station manager and policeman. The Board's managers possessed the power to punish gambling, swearing, drinking alcohol and unauthorised entry; they could enter homes at will, search for goods and people or inspect for cleanliness. Those who wished to be exempted from these demeaning regulations had to apply for a permit, colloquially known as a 'dog-tag', which was very rarely given to an adult still residing on an Aboriginal station. In 1953, in the period when the confrontation described by Mrs Doolan occurred, there were 72 convictions for drunkenness out of a total Aboriginal population of 192. In the same period, only 92 white citizens were charged with any offence out of a total of over 7000, a proportion of one in 2.65 compared to one in 75.[22] It is no coincidence that by far the greatest proportion of Wiradjuri children in the post-war period were removed from Erambie Station. To the overarching purpose of reducing Aboriginality, child-removal now can be added as a tool of community control.

Children

In the institutions

Life in the pre-Second World War institutions was bleak and sterile. Parents could visit their children only once a year, for which arrangements had to be made with the local station manager. After the war the standard of care was undoubtedly better; the Cootamundra Matron tried hard to shield the girls from exploitation in the domestic situations in which they were placed after the age of fourteen or fifteen, but abuses were still common. But she, like most other conscientious white people of her day believed that Aboriginal children had a right to a western education rather than a right to their Aboriginality. In an interview she maintained to me 'Well there wasn't much understanding to do. I mean, there wasn't much difference between Aboriginal children and white children.'[23] That was the voice of reason of the mid-1950s.

Still it was obvious to the children that their Aboriginality was held to be generally inferior: many unconsciously tried hard to become the white people they could not be. Sometimes the mental separation between themselves and any other Aborigine was so strong that they thought they were fundamentally different. Alicia Adams, who was raised in a church home, described the extraordinary psychological effects of the staff's (and society's) labelling of her Aboriginality as inferior. She describes here her relation to 'Mum'—the matron—in the infants home:

> I never knew I had a mother or a father. I just thought Mum [matron] was my mum, you know, my white mum and I thought all the ladies were my real aunties, because they were all white and I really loved them you know, each one of them.

I asked Alicia if she thought she was different from the other children. She answered

> Yes actually I did, and I said to myself, 'These people are different, they're dark', and I thought I was white you see. I said, 'I wonder why they're so dark?' I was looking at my sister Sally and thought, 'Dear she's really black' and you

know, I was really confused. I looked at my skin, and I
thought, 'I look brown like them too', but I said, 'Oh no,
I'm white. . . . And I was real hurt because I didn't want to
be brown, you know, I wanted to be white.[24]

Running away from the homes was common, even if the
girls did not know where they were running to; those who
did not try to escape were still aware that the lonely, affec-
tionless life which they led was not the family life experienced
by white children. One former inmate recalled:

I spent many hours sitting on the fence looking down into
the town, trying to imagine what it was like to live in one
of the homes with a family, or having the freedom to be able
to walk down to the shops, or ride a bicycle around.[25]

Several girls remember the staff telling them 'don't hang
your heads, stand up straight'. It was only as adults that they
realised that it was the staff themselves who, perhaps unconsciously, had taught the children to hang their heads in shame
at their very existence.

The Kinchela Aboriginal Boys Home was altogether a
more brutal institution than Cootamundra Girls Home. A
former inmate told me that he had been tied to an iron frame
and flogged after running away.[26] After 1945 parents were still
discouraged from visiting and the boys were strongly discouraged from returning home. A friend of mine, who used to
work in Link-Up, was told by the superintendent that his
father was dead: the official lied to him to stop him resuming
his Aboriginal identity. Managers believed the boys' intelligence to be typically and naturally low; even those who did
well at school were often described in the Home as 'dull' or
'subnormal';[27] but despite several investigations neither conditions nor amenities improved. The Board, administratively
tucked away in a corner of the Premier's Department, had no

influence on the parliament: far away in Kinchela the lack of financial clout was reflected in the absence of basic children's amenities like a swimming pool or gymnasium.

Note, too, that an Aboriginal boy did not necessarily have to be found unmanageable or delinquent to be placed in Kinchela, merely alleged to be neglected. Yet the staff and even many magistrates behaved as if all the boys were potential criminals. Clarrie Nean, whose sudden death at the Walgett Police Station was investigated by the 1988 Royal Commission into Aboriginal Deaths in Custody, was placed in Kinchela in 1962. (The Royal Commissioner believed that his father's assent form was signed under a form of psychological duress.) After four months Nean absconded to join his family, was caught and went before the Children's Court. At the hearing the magistrate heard evidence that Clarrie hated Kinchela, was teased by the other boys and that the staff were not good to him. The magistrate, however, had visited the Home; he professed himself 'confident and satisfied there was no substance in [Nean's] claim'. For the crime of running away to join his family, Clarrie was sent off to a corrective institution, where he remained for fourteen months.[28] Psychologically he never recovered from the shock of enforced separation.

The Kinchela staff admitted that there was little actual or useful training for the inmates, that the Home was more of a holding station until the boys were sent to the work force.[29] Once on the factory floor, though, very little further interest in them was taken. One former Kinchela inmate, removed from Erambie, recalled:

> We weren't trained for anything. Just go to school, and when you leave school you go as what they call a workman, dairy-boy sort of thing. See we had a big dairy going there . . . It was a training school, but as for getting any training, I

couldn't see it, 'cause no one was skilled in anything, no trades.[30]

Adopted

After the Second World War the cost of maintaining the Kinchela and Cootamundra institutions, as well as new psychologists' theories about the importance of the mother-child bond, caused the Board to seek adoptive and foster parents for its separated children. After 1955 more New South Wales children were placed in white (that is, Anglo-Australian or European-Australian) nuclear families than in the institutions.

Now the children's identity was under a new threat. They might be loved as individuals and family members (though that could not be taken for granted) but they lacked the solidarity of shared Aboriginality which the inmates of the all-Aboriginal children's institutions felt. At least at Kinchela and Cootamundra the inmates were in no doubt that they were Aboriginal! Parents were advised to tell their adopted children that they were of Asian or Greek or Italian descent and to burn the official papers. Sometimes the parents themselves, misinformed by the hospital in which their baby was born, believed this themselves. Though few New South Wales Aborigines of the full-descent survived, it was still held that the assimilation policy was appropriate for part-Aboriginal people because they were not really Aborigines anyway.

It is in these unfortunate circumstances that many children suffered as well. Their sad lives might not necessarily result from a lack of love but from their parents failing to comprehend the depth of antipathy towards their children by the world outside the front gate, or their inability to offer a support network for their children hurt by discrimination or racist slurs, or even their own unconscious antipathy towards Aboriginality.

One 21-year-old woman interviewed for *The Lost Children* was adopted by a white family with very positive feelings towards their child's Aboriginality. The speaker thought her parents 'very good':

> My mother always wanted a little Koori [Aboriginal] baby . . . I think Mum told me [about the adoption] when I was little, and then when I started to worry about it all, she told me again . . . It never really worried me till I was fourteen.[31]

Yet parents like these were unable to help their daughter outside the family home. She went on

> I think it worries you when you start high school. You feel a bit funny. You feel a bit funny being the only black person in a whole pile of whites. I got called 'you black bitch' and stuff like this . . . It makes you feel dirty. Sometimes I'd come home from school and go in my bedroom and I'd cry. I'd think to myself. I wish I could get this skin off me some-how. That's how you feel when all the trouble starts.

An Aboriginal field-worker commented on the inability of white parents to help their children in such circumstances:

> Many white foster parents have been confronted with the problem of finding their children employment, many Aboriginal children have become totally despairing when they're continually refused employment regardless of their qualifications and capabilities . . . Most Aboriginal families are equipped to cope with continual rejection, they have been raised to know prejudice, or rather smell it a mile off, but an Aboriginal child reared by white foster parents would have no idea of the real problem either would the foster parents for that matter . . . As you become older the com-plexities of adult life arise you find some of your white

friends tend to try not to show signs of a past close relationship, especially in front of other white people.[32]

Rather more common than a positive attitude towards Aboriginality was antipathy towards both the natural relations and the Aboriginality of the child. For example, one woman was adopted as a baby to a family which later adopted other Aboriginal children. She believed that the attitude of her white adoptive parents was:

> Very similar to most white people, which is: Aboriginals are drunk, they don't work hard, they go walkabout, they never seem to achieve much.

This woman's brother was placed in substitute care with another family. Although he was fostered, not adopted, he was neither told that he was Aboriginal nor his real name. He recalled an upbringing similar to that of his sister:

> I can remember the foster father used to be a bit of a racist. I remember there used to be a lot on TV about the Aboriginals living in missions and stuff, and they'd just show the shanties, and he'd say, 'Look at these people, they don't get off their arses and help themselves'.

Another woman also suffered from the prejudices of her adoptive parents towards Aborigines:

> My foster parents didn't let me watch TV or anything that had anything Aboriginal, really tried to hide me from my culture. They were racist, and they didn't like anyone who didn't have money or a good job . . . That was Carlingford, upper-class area, really racist. No other Aboriginals in sight, not one. All they had was not their own ideas, but their parents', and society and the media. What's on the front page of the Herald this morning: booze, blacks all the big bad words.

One could argue that these victims of separation suffered from negative attitudes towards their Aboriginality because their substitute parents were not their natural parents, that a biological white parent would not harbour such negative feelings towards their own child. But that doesn't seem to be the case. A man who told his story in the oral history *The Lost Children* was born to an Aboriginal mother and non-Aboriginal father. After his mother died, his father consistently denied not only the boy's Aboriginality, but his mother's as well:

> Although I always suspected it deep down, the first real con-firmation came after I left Burnside [Home]. I would have been about twelve or thirteen years old and my father had remarried and I had gone to live with him and my step-mother. One of my older brothers came to the house with a form to join the army. One of the questions was about nationality and he asked my father if my mother had any 'col-oured' blood in her. I think that was the term he used. My father hit the roof and said, 'As far as I am concerned your mother was white!' And that's where the discussion ended.

The boy's dark complexion, however, made him easily iden-tifiable as Aboriginal:

> In the forties and fifties there was the instilled attitude that Aboriginal people were hopeless cases. That is why, at school, whenever anything came up in class about Aborigines (such as when they attacked the explorers) everybody used to cast accusing glances and I would shrink down in my seat.

It is evident that Aboriginal children may be victims of thoughtless or vindictive racism in school regardless of the wishes or capacity of the white parent. The consequences of a poor self image was that the children became withdrawn, or were forced towards other rejected children in the school such as 'new Australians'. While it is not uncommon today for an Aboriginal child to be the only such child in the class, or even the school, there was, in all the cases outlined above, no support community to reinforce a positive image of Aboriginality. An adopted woman reflected:

> They [adopting parents] were turning me into a white person, they were taking my whole culture and my whole everything from me and making me what they wanted me to be as an adopted child . . . Oh I got heaps at school. 'Abo'. 'Black'. It's really hard if you don't come from a black family, 'cause you can't go home and say, 'Mum they called me an Abo'. If you did she'd say 'Oh the silly white bastards, don't worry about them'. That would have made me feel proud of what I was. But if I went home and said 'They called me an Abo today' my foster parents would either just say nothing or they'd say 'You have to put up with it'. I used to think I was a real reject. I ended up doing bad at school just because of it.

Each of the men and women quoted here found themselves discriminated against in the school or work-place regardless of whether the white family loved and supported them. All found that the family could offer no useful counsel when the inevitable discrimination occurred. Most white parents probably attributed any perceived shortcomings in their child to the 'Aboriginal' side of its nature. Children who ran away from school were often said to have 'gone walkabout', as if truancy needed a different explanation for white and black children. A poor school performance was likely to be explained by 'Well his mother was Aboriginal, what can you expect?' In many cases the child was not even expected to succeed, which set in train a self-fulfilling prophecy of Aboriginal 'backwardness'.

In later life

The children who went out to work generally found that discrimination did not end with school. This woman was working as a receptionist:

> When I was behind the desk a couple of times, people'd walk in and as soon as they saw me they'd go 'Oh! look at you,' and then walk up. Their whole attitude would change. They'd throw the papers at you, but I was never rude.

Thousands never came home and are lost to their families and communities forever. More than once I have been told on the doorstep of a Link-Up client's sister or cousin 'I don't wish to find my family thank you. Goodbye'. Many of those who did, ironically used the skills they gained outside to further the Aboriginal cause. A former Cootamundra inmate declared:

> I [became] Secretary of the Progress Association, 'cause I could write, I suppose, knew a bit about how to run a meeting, must've been from school days. And I thought they didn't know very much about how a meeting should be run. . . . Then I got on a Country Woman's [Association] thing. . . . Next thing I was working in the pre-school there for about five years, and I started reading a lot more then, reading Aboriginal stuff.

Lowitja O'Donoghue, the former Chair of the Aboriginal and Torres Strait Islander Commission and Charles Perkins, the first Aboriginal Secretary of a Commonwealth Government department, were both separated from their communities when children. An informal estimate places the proportion of 1992 national ATSIC Commissioners who were removed as more than three-quarters of the Commission's councillors.

Success at meetings and political organisation comes

invariably at a cost. The removed children have remained, to a greater or lesser extent, on the edge of the firelight of their family's hearth, whatever their achievements in the outside world. Charles Perkins explained:

> You lose things along the way . . . You lose the love of your family and home which some people think are important. I do. You develop a set of values which you are not entirely happy with when you finally achieve some form of success. And is it success in consideration of what you would have done in another world? I would hate anybody to have to live the life I have had to live.

These success stories too easily obscure the histories of the majority of traumatised adults who died young, abandoned their children, beat their wives or children, were unable to maintain constructive lives, committed violent crimes, killed themselves or were driven insane. No national figures are available on the relationship between serious crime and separation, but an indication is provided by the estimate that 90 per cent of the clients seeking assistance from the Victorian Legal Service for criminal charges in 1976 had been in substitute placement at some time in their lives.[33] Even today non-Aboriginal Australia blames serious crimes on Aborigines and enacts legislation specifically (though seldom nominally) aimed at them.[34] The legislators do not seem to appreciate that the situation is one of their own making: it is their own repressive institutions and cruel policies which traumatised the children and rendered many of them unable to take a normal part in adult life.

How can one grapple with the moral complexities of a ghastly crime committed by an Aboriginal stolen while still a child, deprived of love and subjected to brutal discrimination? The singer/songwriter Archie Roach, himself a removed child, intuitively understood. The last verse of his song about

Russell Moore, the Victorian Aboriginal taken to the USA by his adopting parents and later convicted of murder and rape, runs:

> They took you there when you were five
> Now you're in some jail trying to survive
> And if the truth be known when all have testified
> Another crime committed here was genocide.[35]

Permanent trauma is as tragic to the individual as to society. Clarrie Nean, sent by the unthinking magistrate from Kinchela to the reformatory, was an alcoholic long before he died. Malcolm Smith, another former Kinchela and reformatory inmate, killed himself by smashing a paintbrush through his eye and through his brain out of self-hatred while under a religious hallucination.[36] When we read testimonies like those in Chapter 1 we understand that such self-hatred didn't come from nowhere.

The relevance of the assimilation policy today is that, while 'integration' and 'self-determination' are terms thrown off by politicians, the view is still widely held in the community that northern Aborigines are in essence different from southerners, who are not really Aboriginal at all. It is not uncommon for trainee teachers to be told, for instance, that they should learn about Aboriginal culture 'just in case you have to go and teach in the Kimberleys'—as if there were not likely to be Aboriginal children in every primary school in the country.

Aboriginal people have never ceased to maintain that people of traceable Aboriginal descent who wish to identify as Aboriginal are entitled to do so and should be allowed by the courts to do so. The Aboriginal playwright Jack Davis wrote a poem in 1975 'In reply to a statement made by a Minister for Aboriginal Affairs that urban Aborigines were not true Aborigines':

With murder, with rape, you marred their skin,
But you cannot whiten their mind;
They will remain my children forever
The black and the beautiful kind.[37]

3

The Stolen
Generations

In the 1970s I interviewed a number of Aboriginal people
who had been separated, but I listened to them as individuals
without thinking about the effect on Aboriginality as a whole.
In 1980 I began working on a thesis about the Wiradjuri
people of New South Wales and obtained permission to
research the records of the Aborigines Protection Board.
When the Aborigines Protection Board was terminated in
1969, its records were bundled up and placed in the State
Archives. By 1980, no one had any idea of what these records
contained. Though some records are still missing, the extant
quantity was enormous—22,000 files in the General
Correspondence files from 1935 to 1969 alone.

The first records I examined were those of the State
Wards 1916–28, the one-page case summaries of the first 800
Aboriginal children removed from their families after the
1915 amendment to the *Aborigines Protection Act* which
enabled the Protection Board to move against the communities. I was stunned by the off-hand dismissal of so many wards
under the section of the printed form marked 'Disposal', in
which the clerk had written 'Died tuberculosis' or 'Believed

living with a white man' or 'Absconded while in service, current address unknown'.

The Board began to keep longer running files on each ward from about 1933. I began making my way through them, scarcely able to grasp the casual cruelty inflicted upon the children in its direct charge and care, nor the unwillingness of the officials to analyse the comprehensive failure of the separation policy evidenced in their own records. These fat files still secured by a rusting clip, almost invariably trace, through 50 or 60 dusty pages, a child's distressing trauma and sometimes disintegration. I followed the career of one individual after another, between the parameters of 'pleasant and lively' young kiddies, to 'no knowledge of whereabouts' or 'found dead, possibly murdered'. Some end with a birth certificate of a child born to the ward, others with a request for payment of wages. When at length I reached the end of those 700 files, I at last understood that the red herrings of missionary zeal, malnutrition, parental neglect, the best interest of the child and the standards of the day, concealed a violent and premeditated attack not only on Aboriginal family structure but on the very basis of Aboriginality itself. I at last was beginning to grasp what now, in 1999, seems so obvious.

The officials' comments live with me to this day. I still can see 'No answer required' written across a mother's request to see her child. I recall vividly a detailed description of a ward's violent confrontation with her foster parents and their total inability to comprehend the cause. Often able to absorb no more, I used to sit on the grassy slope outside the State Archives Office at Circular Quay, my heart pounding at the import of the records so casually recounting the destruction of a seemingly endless succession of Aboriginal Australians, returning to the desk still shaken, to recount wide-eyed what I had just read to any unfortunate friend or acquaintance who happened to be working at the Archives.

For a decade now the files have been closed to all except the individual concerned or a close relative if deceased. To those individuals whose personal files (with official permission) I read in 1980–81, I can only apologise for such an invasion of their privacy. But I put my time to good use. I made an index that was used for many years by Link-Up clients to track their pasts through their own files. Without reading each one I would have taken much longer to realise their sinister import. Later I had the privileged but chilling experience of sitting with many of the subjects as they painfully re-lived their dreadful lives through the dreadful pages of their personal files.

During that year, 1981, I met a former State Ward, Coral Edwards, who was making a film about her own life at the Australian Institute of Aboriginal Studies. She told me about her life in the Cootamundra Aboriginal Girls Home, and I recounted to her stories of people whom I had met, and the explosive nature of the Protection Board archives. After months of conversation, Coral asked me to accompany her to Tingha, the town from which she had been taken while she still a babe in arms.

In daily contact with a growing number of people still suffering the terrible consequences of separation, and still working through the State Ward files in the State Archives, I wrote the paper on which this chapter revolves at white heat in a single day, still overwhelmed by the nonchalant wickedness vibrating in the dusty silences of the State Archives and the overgrown cemeteries of a hundred outback towns.

I imagined at the time that I was writing the stories of individuals, but I understand now that I was historicising the process of separation. The sum of the 'lazy and useless' domestic servants and alcoholic violent men was more than thousands of difficult, futile or wasted lives. It was the by-product of a concerted attempt by the state to put an end to indigenality. At last I understood the life histories not only as human tragedies, but also the context in which these things were allowed, no, were intended, to happen.

I wrote 'The Stolen Generations' in 1980 at the request of the Family and Children's Service Agency in Sydney.[1] My original title was 'The Lost Generations'. My partner Jay Arthur thought the title a little euphemistic and suggested 'The Stolen Generations'. So it became. She is the author of the phrase, not I. 'The Stolen Generations', (1980):

> In view of the inadequate provision as regards housing, food and care of the children of . . . ., on the Aboriginal reserve at . . . ., would you kindly charge the children as neglected and commit them to the care of this Board'— Letter from Aboriginal Welfare Board to Police Sergeant, at a mid-Western town in New South Wales, 1958.

White people have never been able to leave Aborigines alone. Children particularly have suffered. Missionaries, teachers, government officials, have believed that the best way to make black people behave like white was to get hold of the children who had not yet learned Aboriginal lifeways. They thought that children's minds were like a kind of blackboard on which the European secrets could be written.

This is about what happened to those children who were taken away from their parents from reserves or the bush by government legislation, and put in the care of the whites. It is the story of the attempt to 'breed out' the Aboriginal race. It is the story of attempted genocide.

Genocide does not simply mean the extermination of people by violence but may include any means at all. At the height of the policy of separating Aboriginal people from their parents the Aborigines Welfare Board meant to do just that.

The 1921 Report of the Board stated that 'the continuation of this policy of dissociating the children from camp life must eventually solve the Aboriginal problem'.

'The Aboriginal problem' meant Aboriginal people who could not, or chose not, to live as white people wanted them to do. The 1926 Report put the Board's intentions even more clearly: when children were placed in a 'first class private home', the superior standard of life would 'pave the way for the absorption of these people into the general population'. At the same time, Aboriginal adults, who could not be sent away were driven from reserves or from the outskirts of country towns. Adult Aboriginal resistance proved too strong for the Board, for those adults either came back after a time, or went to live outside another town. But the children could not return until they were eighteen. Some were taken so young that they did not remember where they had come from or even who their parents were. Many of these children did not, and could not, return to their families.

The following story is a composite one, the details taken from the case histories of a number of families. Suppose that, in 1950, a family containing seven children was living on a reserve, when it was learned that an inspector of the Aborigines Protection Board was to pay a visit. Both the children and parents knew from past experience that they might have to fight for the right to stay together. What they did not know was that their names were already on the inspector's blacklist as a family whose lifestyle did not match the manager's[2] opinion of how Aboriginal families ought to live. Nor did they know that a magistrate's committal hearing was scheduled for the following week, nor that the local police had already been asked to prepare a charge sheet for each of the children, as 'neglected and under incompetent guardianship'. Nor did they know that, far away in Cootamundra and

Kempsey, the superintendents had been warned to prepare places for several more children.

A week later the hearing (it was only a formality) was over. The children were committed and not allowed to return home. They were kept in the local hospital, until on the eighth day after the hearing, they were quietly placed on a bus and driven away. No one waved goodbye. No one on the station even knew when they went.

The mother, suddenly deprived of her family, went into a state of shock from which she never really recovered. For months, not a word was heard of her children. In the belief that some of the older children had been placed as domestic servants for white families in Sydney, she bought presents and at Christmas went to Sydney to find them. She never knew whether it was by accident or not that she was sent to the wrong address, but she arrived at a home in Woollahra to find that her daughter had been sent somewhere else. Nobody seemed to know where. Her presents were taken by the children at the place where she was staying, and she arrived home without gifts or information. Meanwhile her husband remained an alcoholic.

The two-year period of the children's detainment came and went without comment from any white official. Then a little information trickled back about what had become of the children. One, it seemed, had died, but nobody knew where or when or how. (In the private files of the Board was the information that she had died of tuberculosis at Waterfall Sanitarium in 1952.)

Two children, it was said, had married white people and raised their children as whites, but that was only a rumour. (The Board's records noted this to be the case and recorded the details of the marriages.) Of the fourth child nothing was heard, beyond that she had been taken to the Bomaderry Children's Home until she was seven, and then a white person from Victoria had taken her away. (That was where the Board's records ended, too.)

Of the fifth child nothing at all was known. He simply disappeared. (The Board's records contained no information, indeed, the only person who might have been able to help was the Superintendent of Bloomfield Mental Hospital, at Orange, who wrote to the Board enquiring about four Aboriginal people, all vague about their past lives, who had been admitted with histories of violence, but who now did not seem to want to leave.) One of the boys eventually came home, now twenty years old. He was alcoholic and refused to talk of his experiences. The seventh child, a girl, came home, too. All she would say was that she had a baby at the Ashfield Children's Home, which was taken away from her when it was two weeks old, and she had never seen it again. She married a local man, and lived at the reserve.

As the children who had come back grew to their thirties, it was clear that they were not able to function as normal adults. They had nightmares. They resented their parents, particularly their mother, as if she had been responsible for their removal. They had periods of alcoholism during which they became uncontrollably violent. They drank or gambled what few wages they earned and remained what the Aborigines Protection Board called 'unassimilable'.

The family is imaginary, but every one of the details happened to one or more individuals. Yet the policy which allowed such events to take place was proposed, debated and affirmed in the parliament of the state of New South Wales, and for 50 years was sanctioned and administered by the Aborigines Protection (later Welfare) Board.[3] For two or three generations there was scarcely a word of protest by those whose duty it was to protect: members of parliamentary oppositions, Christians, parents, people of common humanity.

Why? Why was it necessary to remove over 5000 children from their parents and try to turn them into white people?

To quote the words of the Board itself, it was to counter the 'positive menace to the State' which people of Aboriginal descent were supposed to offer the whites. The solution seemed to lie in making people adopt the same values, believe in the same things. The whites could not tolerate a different way of life. They did not like being not wanted, not needed. But legally, economically, and in values, Aborigines were not like whites, and most did not want to be. Those who wanted to be were not allowed to be. When it became obvious that Aborigines didn't want them, or want to be like them, the whites resorted to force.

The first official power over children granted to the Board was through the *Aborigines Protection Act 1909*.[2] Before that, it had to rely on unofficial powers like stopping the food rations to parents whose children did not attend school. Then when the girls' dormitory was built at Warangesda Aboriginal Station on the Murrumbidgee in 1893, the plan was that Aboriginal girls from all over the state would go there to learn how to become domestic servants.

There were no legal powers to coerce people, and since Aborigines showed no enthusiasm for the scheme, the Board resorted to threats and promises. For instance, parents who allowed their girls to go into the dormitory were allowed to stay on Warangesda Station. Those who wanted to leave were offered free rail passes if they left the girls behind. Those who wanted to remove the whole family from the station to avoid the manager's control were warned that they thereby rendered their children liable to prosecution under the *Neglected Children and Juvenile Offenders Act.*

Meanwhile, the boys in the family were simply ordered off Warangesda to find work. Under the new legislation of 1909 children could be removed without their parents' consent only if they were found by a magistrate to be 'neglected'. To the Board's officers, the most useful part of the official definition of 'neglect' was the part dealing with children having 'no visible means of support or fixed place of abode'. Thus parents who were forced to leave Aboriginal stations, or who left their houses on reserves voluntarily in order to retain their children, might be brought before a magistrate for neglecting their children.

However, a practical difficulty was that children were sometimes released by magistrates who reasoned, quite rightly, that well fed and well dressed children could not be considered 'neglected' even if they did live in a tent beside a river. Within a few years of the passing of the *Aborigines Protection Act*, members of the Board were complaining in the annual reports of the inadequacy of their powers. By 1912 the Board was no longer content with its Act.

Three years later the Board's efforts were rewarded with an amendment to the Act which stated that any Aboriginal child might be removed without parental consent if the Board considered it to be in the interest of the child's moral or physical welfare. It was up to the parents to show that the child had a right to be with them, not the other way round. No court hearings were necessary; the manager of an Aboriginal station, or a policeman on a reserve or in a town might simply order them to be removed. The racial intention was obvious enough for all prepared to see, and some managers cut a long story short when they came to that part of the committal notice, 'Reason for Board taking control of the child'. They simply wrote, 'being Aboriginal'.

The 1915 amendment also allowed much younger children than previously to be taken away. The Cootamundra Girls Home was established in 1911 in anticipation of the amendment—it was for those girls too young to go straight into domestic service. (The Kinchela Boys Home was established at Kempsey in 1924. Boys were sent there before being sent out as 'apprentice' farm labourers.) In 1916 the Board began to remove children from their families under the new legislation. A new book called the *Register of Wards* was begun, which contained the details of each commitment and the later history of each ward. Today it is in the State Archives, and in it, even the casual reader may catch a glimpse of the enormous tragedy of what happened to the first 800 children removed under the 1915 amendment.[4]

The law remained as it was until 1939, when Aboriginal children were again brought under the jurisdiction of a new *Child Welfare Act*. Magistrates' hearings before committal again became necessary, but a new category appeared in that Act under which children could be removed from their families. In addition to being 'neglected', children could also be found to be 'uncontrollable': an Aboriginal child who refused to go school, for instance, could be considered 'uncontrollable', and in fact as many children were removed under the new legislation as had been under the *Aborigines Protection Act*.

The 'uncontrollable' clause could be used to separate 'difficult' children from their families, or to transfer children already placed. Since there were no homes set aside specifically for 'uncontrollable' Aboriginal children, children so committed generally went to a state corrective institution like the Parramatta Girls' Home, or Mt Penang. There, their Aboriginality, perhaps denied by the staff and inmates if they were of light colouring, was even more under threat if they were at Kinchela or Cootamundra.

White children too were charged with neglect, and removed from their parents. But the Act under which white children were charged was a good deal more generous in the alternatives it offered to permanent separation, for it was framed for a different purpose. White single mothers could apply for a pension to look after their own children. Children could be committed to a suitable relative, and they could be returned to their parents after a period of good behaviour. Institutionalised children could be returned home for holidays. No such provisions existed under the *Aborigines Protection Act*, for its intention was to separate children from their parents (and their race) permanently. The different attitudes underlying black and white child welfare legislation can be seen by comparing this extract from a report on the Parramatta Industrial Home (1921):

> Just as life is opening before them with all its possibilities of joy and happiness, something happens, and all the 'promise fair' vanishes, and they find themselves walking down that dark and gloomy labyrinth which leads to all that is wrong and bad in life, all that taps the best in their young souls, and all that means in the end, much sorrow and misery.

and this extract from the Report of the Aborigines Welfare Board of 1911:

> to allow these children to remain on the Reserve to grow up in comparative idleness in the midst of more or less vicious surroundings would be, to say the least, an injustice to the children themselves, and a positive menace to the State.

The most important factor in the view of the Board was that Aboriginal children had to be separated from the rest of their race. One annual report of the 1920s predicted that the children, once institutionalised, would not be allowed to return to any Aboriginal station or reserve, 'except perhaps those who have parents, on an occasional visit'. In practice no home visits were allowed at all. Parents received no encouragement to come, and were positively discouraged if they attempted to stay more than a day. Even Christmas holidays were generally spent in the homes. Letters in and out were censored. Brothers and sisters might see each other only every two or three years, often not at all. Children who left the homes for employment were generally forbidden to return, even if it was the only home they knew. That was the one method of separation—to cut off the outside world. The other was propaganda from within. Little by little the view was put across that blacks on reserves were dirty, untrustworthy, bad. There were generally no black staff to whom the children could relate.

Partly because it was presented with no opposition, the propaganda had its successes. Some children left the homes ashamed of the colour of their skin. Girls have stated that they used to cross the road in order to avoid an Aboriginal man, not just because they had been taught to, but because in the end, they themselves had come to believe that he was a threat—dirty, brutal, black!

The staff at the homes varied between those who might have been good in another environment, and the psychopathic. The better ones took an interest in the children, they were called 'mum' or 'dad', and tried to overcome a sterile and hostile environment. But their horizons were lowered in living from day to day, they were over-worked, and probably all of them were brutalised by the system in which they had chosen to work.

What can be said of the good officials is that during their care the children did not suffer more than they had to, and may have suffered less, under a system which was barbaric in its execution and indefensible in its intent. The bad officials were monsters. For instance, after an enquiry in 1935, the manager of Kinchela was warned in a private letter on a number of counts. He must not be drunk on duty. He must no longer use a stockwhip on the boys, nor tie them up. He was not to use dietary punishments. He had to keep a punishment register and he was no longer allowed to send the boys out as labour on local farms. The evidence of some of the boys bears out the enquiry's findings. One man stated that he was kept locked up in a shed for several days and told to eat hay. Another in 1981 had scars on his feet, which he received forty years ago from frost bite, bringing in the cows, without shoes, on winter mornings before dawn.

The brutality of some of the officials was compounded by the lack of external control. Despite the enquiry's findings, the management at Kinchela does not seem to have changed for the better. Eight years later there was another enquiry into what the Board called 'sexual deviance'. An inspector from the Child Welfare Department thought that the boys were bored, even though they had too much manual work to do. Though the manager had conceded that the scrubbing and washing that the boys had to do was not the life of normal healthy boys, the inspector thought that his estimate of the boys' two hours work a day after school was too low.

The boys in reality, he thought, had to work four hours, and in winter they had no time for leisure at all. He noted the pathetic eagerness that the boys showed in helping some workmen mend a wall. One sentence was particularly chilling, as it brings to mind images of prisoners in a concentration camp: 'there is a noticeable tendency for the boys to sit on their haunches motionless and silent'. Sexual deviation, he concluded, sprang very largely from the boys' environment.

Whether the superintendents were good or bad, nothing could change the sterility of the environment. The children were emotionally, spiritually, intellectually and psychologically deprived, and the scars might never heal. In a mid-western town I met an ex-Kinchela man. When he was ten he had been taken straight from school by a welfare officer, he said, and was never able to say goodbye to his father. He was placed in Kinchela and was an inmate during the period described above. He could not, or would not, talk of his experiences there. He was divorced, had been an alcoholic, and was deeply unhappy. I saw him one morning unable to decide whether to go to the doctor or chemist for advice on one of the many ailments with which his life seemed to be preoccupied. Kinchela crippled that man for life.

As the children approached the age of fourteen or fifteen the question arose of their employment. The girls at Cootamundra were better prepared for the work—described by one of them as 'slavery'—for their training in the home coincided exactly with what was needed to be done anyway. It consisted of the scrubbing, washing, ironing and sewing that the Board did not want to pay anyone to do. The same argument did not apply so well to the boys, but they still had to perform scrubbing and kitchen duties anyway, or else they worked in the vegetable gardens or dairy.

In choosing a position, the Board assumed that blacks were stupid. Its very first report in 1883 stated that black children after training would 'take their places with the industrial classes of the colony'. In 1938, 50 years later, it was the same: boys would become rural workers and most of the girls, domestic workers. Such were the advantages of life in white society! Talent was ignored. One boy was noted by the Kinchela manager to enjoy 'sitting by himself for hours playing the mouth organ'. There was no thought of a possible musical career. Although he was noted to have been partic- ularly fond of animals, he was sent to work in the abattoirs of a sheep station. When he ran away, he was charged with being 'uncontrollable'. Today he is a professional musician.

There was a space on a child's term report on which the manager or matron estimated the level of intelligence. Any- thing above 'average' was rare, and the majority ranged from 'poor' to 'moronic'. Sometimes the estimate of the manager was in defiance of a good school report. One child came seventh out of a class of 23, yet the Cootamundra matron characterised her intelligence as 'very, very poor'. One Kinchela manager was questioned about the difference between his low estimate of a boy's ability and the good estimate of Kempsey High School. His reply was simply that the boy appeared unintelligent to him. There seems to have been no comprehension of the effect of environment upon measured intelligence. Many children's marks after a promising start went from bad to worse, and culminated in the remark, 'in view of the low mental capacity of this child I recommend that he does not continue at High School but be sent to employment'.

It was the same with personality. The children were expected to have problems because they were black, and when problems arose, they seemed to confirm the deep-seated notions of racial inferiority. If children ran away from home, it was only to be expected that they would go on walkabout. If they were violent or passive, sullen or outspoken, it was often written down to the unfortunate racial characteristics of the Aboriginal people. The children, and the race itself, were held in the utmost contempt even by some members of the Board. During the enquiry of 1933 into the manager's behaviour, one Board member exclaimed when he heard some of the allegations (there is a verbatim account of the meeting), 'the evidence of these black boy is not worth the paper it is written on'.

At fifteen, the children had to leave the homes, and as State Wards enter an 'apprenticeship'. They might be sent to a pastoral station or to a middle-class home in Sydney. A few (I have not heard of many) were treated with some dignity and respect in their employment. More frequently they became just the little black maid or station hand about the place. They were paid little, and most of that went into a trust account to which access was difficult. (The official reason for this was that it taught wards responsibility, but it could also be used for controlling the way in which money was spent. Request for funds to travel home for a holiday, for instance, could be met with refusal.) Comments by employers, and there are scores of them on the files, indicated a total lack of interest in, or failure to comprehend, the history of individual wards. Phrases like:

> I asked for a trained mission boy and this one cannot do anything.

and, after a boy ran away:

> If you cannot find him within a few days please send a replacement as we need some extra labour for the harvest.

indicate that the Board was sending wards to places that were entirely unsuitable. Children who misbehaved or ran away were sent to some remote station (Brewarrina was a favourite). Just as there was no conception of the real causes of abnormal behaviour in the homes, so there was none when the children were placed in employment. Deceit, laziness, theft, malicious damage, violence and insolence were common complaints.

Nor did employers show any awareness that there may have been deeper factors underlying the confrontation between two individuals. When wards threatened their employers with a broom or carving knife there may have been an element of racial defiance. A descendant of the Indigenous people was threatening a member of the invading race. For white people seem seldom to have realised, let alone acknowledged, that the battle for Australia was the same kind of war of dispossession that was fought by Europeans anywhere in the world. Nor have they realised that military conquest did not necessarily imply psychological defeat. This is a letter from an ex-ward written to his younger brother in service on a pastoral station:

> Listen . . . if you don't like the place where you are working, tell them that you want to get another job, or go to the police station and tell them that you are not getting a fair go and if they don't get you another job first sit down all day and when the boss tells you to do something tell him to shut up. This is what I done when I was in the homes. I will kick his gut out if he doesn't give you a fair go. I'll be down about the seventh of June don't let them white cunts boss you about. I give cunts all they wanted and even told their wife to get stuffed so don't forget . . .

Shortly after receiving this letter, the boy ran away to join his brother. The letter was extracted illegally from the possessions he had left behind, and sent to the Board as evidence of the brother's complicity. Yet the most extraordinary part of the story was to come. The Superintendent of the Welfare Board himself wrote to the policeman at the brother's town. He asked him to tell the brother to write no more letters, or he would be in 'very serious trouble'. The action of the Superintendent and the policeman were technically legal. As well as showing that the Board frequently acted as the agent of repression and control over an invaded people, the incident transcended the confrontation between individuals. It was the centuries old battle between the victor and the victims.

That was in the 1950s. At the same time as this letter was written, Australian primary school children were learning of the heroic exploits of one Andreas Hofer, an obscure European who defended his native land against an invader. They might just as well have looked out the school room doors.

In 1957 the Board placed advertisements in the major

newspapers calling for foster parents to look after Aboriginal children. The principal reason was economic. Children were still being committed in large numbers, yet the Aboriginal institutions were overcrowded. There was an extraordinary response and in a few years more children were in foster care than in the two homes combined.

In many cases, the children were treated kindly, but the pressure on children to make them want to behave like Europeans was enormous. This was especially true for children taken from their families so young that they had no yardstick with which to measure the propaganda. The following unthinking, racist assumptions were contained in a letter written by a woman a few days after she had taken control of a ward:

> The wee girlie has settled down with us very well. She is a charming child and we are already much attached. I took her to the shop and bought jodhpurs, lemon cardigan, shoes, hair-ribbon, gloves and many things I thought she would like. Her eyes fairly sparkled. I think she looks best of all in the school uniform, and we are to buy a navy and white hat with a badge. She also has a hair styling and is a very obedient and affectionate child. Here I must say that Lillian from henceforth would like to be known as Mary Rose, and it is just what I will call her . . .
>
> I was very pleased to notice how modest she is about her person. She is saying her prayers also. She wanted Him to make her 'my colour' (i.e., white). Poor little girl. I explained that God had made men in lots of colours and she seemed much happier then.

This preposterous nonsense contained the seeds of incalculable harm, not least from the expectations sown in the girl's mind that she should in fact be accepted by white people. The great majority of wards, like the great majority of Aborigines, were not accepted as equals by whites.

The subsequent history of this child was sadly typical of a great many Aboriginal children fostered by white people who, whatever their motives, understood nothing of the complexity of raising a child belonging to another race. The girl at the age of eleven began to exhibit the usual behaviour of a child only partially accepted into a foster home and already aware of rejection by the wider society. By the age of twelve her foster mother had rejected her, and, at thirteen, using her own name by choice, she was an inmate of the Cootamundra home. At the time of her transfer, a welfare officer belatedly admitted that the foster mother had been a bad choice. Yet it was the Board which had chosen her in the first rush of publicity, and its officers had been caught in the same affected middle-class vice. This is the summing up of a Board official's inspection of a potential foster parent:

> New home, beautifully furnished, all furniture is modern style made by husband. New Australian Dutch family. Lovely children, very well mannered. This seems ideal for small girl. Better surroundings could not be found. Recommended.

At the age of eighteen, wards and foster children were free legally to do what they wished. A good many went home to an emotional reunion, only to find, if their family lived on a managed Aboriginal station, that they were subject to a whole new set of regulations. If there was no work on the station, and if they were female this was almost certain to be the case, they would have to leave again after a short holiday to find work. If they married, they would be allowed to live on the station, but in practice there were not many men of marriageable age about. They were at Kinchela, or, returning, had been forced to seek work elsewhere. If the young couple married off the station, they were subject to the provisions of the Act by which they had separated from their own parents.

Some went back to bad homecomings, the family dead or moved away. A few—perhaps more than a few—never went back. To help those who wished to return to their families, but were too frightened, and to help parents and children to find each other, an organisation, Link-Up, began in 1981. Several people have, through this service, been reunited with their families. One woman was introduced to her nephew, which appeared to be the first contact she had had with her family for 57 years. Another woman was amazed to learn that twenty years ago she had been returned to Cootamundra by a foster parent for reasons she stated were totally fictitious. It was another case of rejection by the foster parent when the child reached puberty. A third person went back to a mid-western town to find her family at the age of thirty. She had been a foster child, and, she said, had visited every town in New South Wales except the one she knew to be her birthplace. She had until then been too frightened to return, for she had to come to grips not only with a new set of relatives, but with her own Aboriginality from which she had been estranged for so long. Many adults have yet to return, and need encouragement.

The force of white propaganda about 'dirty blacks' including, by implication, a person's own parents, has proved too strong for many who were taken too young to be aware of what they had lost. Those that did go back found a very different world from that which they had been told to expect. They had been told that southern Aborigines had no culture. Once they stopped speaking their language, and dancing their corroboree, somehow they were Aborigines no longer. The late Professor Elkin, a member of the Board and the official anthropological adviser for many years, must carry some of the blame for this. In 1944 he wrote:

The mixed blood people, however, have been in the unfortunate position of possessing no social life worth the name. Dotted about in small groups on Reserves and Settlements . . . they have not shared in the general community life, nor have they any traditional or spontaneous life of their own.

A black writer exclaimed that 'the denial of culture to southern Aborigines is the final colonial insult'. Yet this opinion, so deeply ingrained in the minds of the white population, was the foundation of the Assimilation Policy. The whites were so mesmerised by their own view of society that they could not perceive the value of alternative child raising methods, which were an integral part of the 'non-existent' black culture. One official wrote that the children of a certain woman at La Perouse should be seized because she kept leaving them with relatives for hours while she went shopping. He must have been unaware that leaving children with extended kinfolk had been common since the white invasion, and probably for thousands of years before that. No granny, according to the whites, no cousin or auntie, could look after the children as well as the parents. As soon as the parents ceased to look after their children in the manner approved by officials, there was the opportunity for the children to be removed. In a small country town on the western slopes, the mother of a family died on 8 February 1948. On the 14th, her four children were committed on the grounds of 'incompetent guardianship, no-one to look after the children'. Proceedings must have begun almost on the day of the mother's death. Obviously no attempt at all was made to find a relative to look after the children. By the time relatives in other towns heard what had happened it would have been too late. It was more than a question of the Board simply not trying to find someone. Most of the officers did not approve of auntie, or grandmother, or grandmother's brother, looking after the children. Black children had to be brought up in the approved way, or the state would take them.

Many ex-wards, especially women, resent criticism of the institutions. They argue that if they had been left on the reserves they would now be barefoot, pregnant or drunk. Through the homes, they say they have gained a knowledge of the 'right' way of life.

The psychological issues in the institutionalisation of the children are most complex, and I shall not pursue the subject except to make two points. One is that very few indeed of the ex-institution people have been, in fact, accepted by the whites as equals. No amount of 'white' behaviour or attitudes can overcome skin-colour, or restore dignity to one's self-concept. The other is that people who accepted the white culture as superior will not readily admit to the whites' crime of trying to 'breed out' the Aboriginal race.

Other products of separation can also be recognised. One is the large group of people who will not talk of their experiences at all. Their refusal to talk tells its own story. The alcoholics too tell a story without words, as do the ex-wards who, deprived of parental caring behaviour as children, later abandoned their own children. Every one of the 5000 children removed from their parents had, and has, their own private and bitter memories of separation and later problems of adjustment. From the point of view of the Aboriginal race as a whole, we can hardly guess at the cost of wasted talent of those who spent a decade in the service of the whites. We can hardly guess at the number of men and women who deny their own birth-right as Aboriginal citizens of Australia. The comparisons must tell the story. Perhaps one in six or seven Aboriginal children have been taken from their families during this century, while the figure for white children is about one in three hundred. To put it another way, there is not an Aboriginal person in New South Wales who does not know, or is not related, to one or more of his/her countrymen who were institutionalised by the whites.

The whites tried to justify their actions in various ways. First that there were inspectors, officials and regulations to protect the children from abuse. Yet Margaret Tucker, in her book *If Everybody Cared*, wrote that she was too frightened to complain about her employer to the 'homefinder', and so she stayed in the employ of a cruel and brutal sadist. Probably that was a common enough story. Bad regulations must be challenged, otherwise safeguards in the legal system are worthless. Thus the depriving of rations to parents who did not send their children to school was surely illegal, but no one challenged the regulations and the practice continued. Good regulations too must be enforced, or they are worthless. Thirty years after the enquiry into the Kinchela manager's abuse of his power, another manager was found to have administered ten strokes of the cane on the bare buttocks of a boy for 'sexual perversion'. Yet his reprimand was the same as it had been in 1933: a private letter telling him not to do it again.

Another justification was that the children were in dire need, deserted by their parents and family, or committed to the homes by their own parents. I have already discussed the Board's lack of effort to find relatives willing to look after the children. And we can only guess at the pressure applied by welfare officers when they wrote on the file, 'I have been trying to persuade Mr. and Mrs . . . . to commit their children to the care of the Board'. What threats, what inducements were offered, the children never knew. Today as adults they feel only the hurt of 'my mother put us away'. Almost always there was more to the story than the official version. One family lost seven children to the Board all at once, and the reason was put down to the fact that the parents had deserted their children. The story the mother told was this: she had gone on a holiday and left the children in the care of their grandmother. Food was short, and the grandmother applied for food relief, as the mother herself had done frequently. The welfare officer heard of the case, and the children were removed.

Another justification was that it was in the children's own interest to be taken. Two beds for six children, food kept in a suitcase, even an unweeded garden were taken as signs that the parents were incompetent. In one case a relative offered to look after four committed children. A policeman (a probationary constable) visited the home, and his report ran, 'Mrs . . . . agreed that she did not have sufficient accommodation to look after the extra children'. Comment is scarcely necessary on the status of the woman's agreement. When we consider the question of parental desertions more generally, it seems that the practice is so painful that only extraordinary circumstances can lead people to do it: enforced residence on a station run like a concentration camp, and alcoholism caused by poverty and hopelessness would be two such factors.

Last of all is the excuse 'we didn't know'. But there was adequate opportunity to know. In the Second Reading Debate on the 1916 amendment to the *Aborigines Protection Act*, which gave the Board almost unlimited powers to remove Aboriginal children, one member of parliament spoke against it. He denounced the suggested scheme as slavery. There would be mean officials, he predicted, cringing, crawling, merciless, grasping, cruel officials, not humanitarian but who just obeyed the letter of the law, in league with the local squatters who just wanted cheap labour. Girls who were taken would be exposed to more vice than if they had stayed in the camps. Improve the children if you can, he said, but you will not improve a child by taking it away from its parents. The separation of a swallow from its parents was cruelty. Yet the amendment was carried by 28 votes to three.

Ignorance is no defence. The whites were so convinced of the rightness of their own way of life that they excluded all the others. So deep was the idea of the worthlessness of Aboriginal society in New South Wales that hardly anybody, from the highest level of administration to the lowest, got past the old irrelevancies that they respected or were friendly with certain Aborigines. What was required was an appreciation of Aboriginal lifeways in their own right, not as lived by particular individuals. Most of the officials did not arrive at the starting point, that is, the recognition of the existence of New South Wales Aboriginal culture, let alone take the second step, which was to acknowledge its validity.

The blacks whose families remained intact have known all along what the Board was trying to do, and why. For generations Aborigines have suffered. Perhaps in time the whites will suffer in the knowledge of what they have done. But they cannot expect forgiveness.

By the early 1980s the Stolen Generations themselves were beginning to grasp that the actual motivations for removal bore very little resemblance to those reasons in which they had been indoctrinated. Coral Edwards, who had travelled to Tingha in search of her own Aboriginality, shared that understanding. Following her own journey to her birthplace, she now proposed that she and I establish an organisation to enable others who had suffered, like herself, to find their way home. I agreed and we began to plan what would be needed. She called the new organisation Link-Up.

4

'Like being born all over again' The establishment of Link-Up

In 1983 the Aboriginal communities still had not regained their understanding of child separation as central to their history. A turning point was an address which Coral Edwards made to the National Aboriginal Consultative Council meeting in Canberra soon after the Labor government had been elected. Coral asked for a hearing by the Council, and Ossie Cruse, one of the senior New South Wales representatives, found her a place on the agenda. Forty mostly middle-aged Aboriginal community leaders, each one touched to a lesser or greater degree by the still unfathomed separation policy, wondered at the significance of her topic 'Link-Up'.

Coral took the podium at the head of a horseshoe-shaped conference table. She began to discuss some of our recent work. 'Mothers didn't give their children away', she explained, 'that's just what the children were told.' Cousins had been indoctrinated into feelings of inferiority. Brothers and sisters had not come back because they thought themselves too flash but because they were ashamed of their own skin colour. Most important, *the governments never intended that the children should ever return.*

It was one of those remarkable moments when Australian history takes a new direction. A palpable silence descended on the smoky atmosphere. Heads looked up, pencils hovered. Unspoken questions began to flash about the room: 'Is that why I've never met my auntie?' 'Is that why my family never talks about my youngest sister?' 'Do you mean that my mother didn't put us away?' Twenty five minutes was enough. The NACC voted Link-Up $5000 immediately and recommended to the Minister for Aboriginal Affairs that full-time funding be found for the organisation. Link-Up was formally established.

Link-Up's purposes were first to find out where our client's family were living, second to arrange a meeting with them, and lastly to do what we could to help maintain continuing good relations with that family. In 1983, although we had already been working with former inmates of the Cootamundra and Kinchela Home for some time, we began to work formally with our first clients.

We quickly came to recognise that the questions asked by prospective clients had tended to be similar—obvious when I reflected on the commonality of experience which our clients had shared, and obvious also in the hopes and fears that they brought to their quest. The questions are still being asked. I wrote this pamphlet of questions and answers in 1983 for the use of the early Link-Up clients.

How can Link-Up help me?

The effect on Koori children separated from their

families and raised by whites takes many forms. A few—and they are the lucky ones—go on to lead happy and well-adjusted lives. More often as adults they experience curiosity, uncertainty, unhappiness, depression or permanent alienation. A large proportion of Kooris, we still don't know how large, who are in prison or mental hospitals, were removed from their families when they were little. Link-Up doesn't believe that all Kooris raised by whites are, or ought to be, unhappy. But we do appreciate that the effects of separation take many forms. There are as many individual problems of how to come to terms with the past as there are people suffering. There is one thing you have in common—the long years of uncertainty, the dark hole inside that can't be filled without knowing who you really are.

Yet, though each story is an entirely personal one, we also see the thousands of Aboriginal adults in search of their identity as part of a bigger question of Aboriginal identity in Australia. We estimate that there have been about 8000 children in New South Wales who not only missed out on their family life but on being Aborigines as well. People of Aboriginal descent but who don't identify as Aboriginal, and maybe don't even know that they are Aboriginal, are obviously not Aborigines in the full sense of the word. Therefore, the adults who have not yet made contact with their families are an enormous loss to us as self-identifying Aborigines. To put it another way, all this century, one in six Aborigines have not been allowed to grow up proud that they are Aboriginal. Helping these adults re-establish their identity is one of the most important tasks in Aboriginal Australia today. We make up less than 3 per cent of the population, and if we can help one more Koori regain that pride, there is one more Koori in the state. Mary, an early client of Link-Up, put it in a nutshell when she met her family for the first time in 22 years. She said, 'it was like being born all over again'.

It was not simply some accident of history that our children were taken away to be raised by whites. It was part of deliberate government policy to separate as many Kooris as possible from each other. For this reason we believe that the search for the 'real self' has a sharper edge to it even than the problems of white children who were fostered or adopted. The records of the stolen children, whether they are in the State Archives (where all the old government records are kept) or in church homes, are *our* records. Although it is only you who have the right of access to the file that was kept on you, we see all those records, taken together, as just as much Aboriginal property as the boomerangs and spears in glass cases in museums. At present, by law, an adopted person has no right to information about the natural family. Link-Up believes that when you are denied this information, it is not only you who suffers, but the whole Koori community. *You are being prevented from becoming an Aborigine.*

How and why were the children taken away?

The short answer is that for the last 100 years government policy has been to break up the association of Koori people with each other. The government was given the power to drive people off reserves, to bull-doze fringe-camps, offer nice houses in town with white neighbours on each side and to divide people into meaningless categories like 'quarter-caste' and 'quadroon'. The most sinister power was the one which allowed children to be removed without their parents' consent; sinister because it was clothed with the most elaborate nonsense about how children on reserves were 'a positive menace to the state', how their parents were 'incapable' and how the reserves themselves were an 'immoral influence'. In the Act the official causes for removing children were that they were considered 'neglected' or 'uncontrollable' but in practice most officials simply believed that it was undesirable for Aboriginal children to remain with their parents—undesirable for the state and, somehow, for the children themselves. In a number of cases people living in country towns were so con-vinced that they were doing the children a favour that they didn't bother going through the legal pro-cess at all. This is what happened to a man, who we'll call John, in 1957:

> Auntie, she remembers it well. Apparently I was
> taken to Sunday school down on the mission and
> these people, they took me out and I was supposed

75

to be going on a holiday or something. Everything was supposed to be fixed up with dad and everyone else, but when I didn't turn up [after Sunday school] dad came down looking for me. Apparently he cut loose, went off his brain and found out that those missionaries took me. Dad, he was really concerned he didn't know anything about it. When I got back to my real family it was 25 years later. [Five years after John was taken] Dad was asked to have me adopted, he completely refused it. He said no.

What was the effect of the separation? It wasn't very unusual for Koori children to be raised by relatives other than their parents. (That was one of the things that the whites found so hard to understand.) What was unusual was that, when welfare officials took the children, the parents didn't know where they were, and the children never came back. What was worse, in the Aboriginal institutions the children learned to be ashamed that they were black. Sometimes as they grew older, girls would cross the street rather than pass an Aboriginal man. The children in foster or adoptive homes generally had different experiences. The new parents told them what they thought or hoped was true, that whites would always accept an Aboriginal person. They reasoned that if they treated their child as an equal, the rest of society would too. The real world was different. As the children reached twelve or thirteen they found that some of their friends, as they began to realise that they were Aboriginal, began dropping away. It became harder to get a friend of the opposite sex. Feeling unwanted and alienated, the children couldn't withdraw into Koori company on the reserves like their cousins back home.

Yet, though their experiences were different, both the children from the institutions and in family care shared the same problems. Very few children, as they grew older, were in fact treated by the whites as their equals. Not accepted by the whites, too ashamed to join the blacks, all too often the Stolen Generations were left in the middle.

But I wasn't stolen—my mother put me away

What the Welfare Board did to Kooris in the name of their 'welfare' is one of this country's best kept secrets. There were so many reasons that could induce or force a natural mother to 'sign away' her children. In hospital the nursing sister could tell a mother that she was being selfish in not signing her child over to a nice, respectable middle-class home. A trick used by welfare officers was to tell the parents that if they signed their children over voluntarily, they would have a better chance of seeing them again soon. Another was to expel a family from a reserve on the grounds that they were 'not Aborigines' (that is, too fair), or unemployed, or disrespectful to the manager. Then the parents would be told a few months later that their children were being removed because they didn't live in a proper house! It was not unknown for a white de facto husband to threaten to throw the whole family out of his house unless his wife 'signed away' the children of a previous marriage.

That's one answer. The other is that children, whether in institutions or families, were generally told the worst possible explanations of why they came to be removed. Telling the children the truth, so it was argued, would make the children more likely to want to find their natural parents. As John related, his father refused to allow him to be adopted. But John was never told this. He grew up believing that nobody cared for him, that his family had just given him away. Another person had the same kind of experience. It was not until she was able to read her own file in the State Archives that she realised that her relatives had tried to have her and her brothers and sisters released from the institutions on four separate occasions. Naturally, the authorities refused. The children were never told how much they were loved and missed.

Our answer to people who worry that their Aboriginal families didn't want them is to say this: it could be that your mother didn't want you, but it's much more likely that pressure was put upon her by some Board or welfare officer. Even if there wasn't direct pressure, you have to remember just how bad conditions on a reserve could be 30 or 40 years ago, how demoralised people could become living under a brute of a manager in a leaking, windowless house with no food, unemployment or welfare benefits. Furthermore, there's probably more to the story than you've been told. Hard though it is, try not to judge your people until you know the full story.

If the ex-wards know where they come from, why don't they go home of their own accord?

Many people have, and are now living happy lives. The ones who have not are sometimes too frightened, as John explains:

> Well in my case I was plain scared. Didn't know what reaction I was going to get if I did go back. I was just more or less scared. It was a crazy feeling.

In many cases there was more to it than a fear of rejection. Children who grew up separated from their fellow Kooris took on the prejudices of the whites because there was no one to contradict them. One woman with whom Link-Up is currently working was put in the Parramatta Girls Home in the 1930s. She remembers that she and the half-dozen Aboriginal girls there were not allowed to mix with other Kooris. Whenever she tried to, the message was reinforced that she must mix only with whites:

> I can remember an Aboriginal man, two Aboriginal men, two of them doing the work [on the road just outside the home] and of course one sung out and asked how we was. And straight away we were marched back in that door, and it was the first day in twelve months that I came outside the walls of Parramatta.
>
> [Q]: *For talking to a Koori?*
>
> Yes, and that's when they told us when they took us back in there we were forbidden, even if we went for a job, that if we see them across the road we were never

to speak to them because they were dirty, they were drunkards, we were to keep away from their house. We were no more Kooris—blackfellows—we were now white people and we were brought up decent, respectable, and we were to forget that black life, because it was filthy.

After she left the institution she was still not allowed to associate with her own people:

When I first came out to my work I never had the opportunity to see any of my Aboriginal Koori girls . . . Every other job I worked at [except one] we were kept right away from any other Aboriginal person, because we'd never seen town. We never seen town to be able to associate with our people, and this is what the [white] people have got to understand, and they took us and hurt our souls. If the mistress went to town we were left at home. If they thought they'd take you once to the pictures, you went with her and her husband and you sit with them. You never left their side . . . that is how they kept us away. That was no accident. Now I've learned all this, years later. If only I had learned it while I was a young woman, and with the strong willpower that I've got now. This is what's making me fight, because I think it's time that the world learned how we felt and how we were broken down in our will-power, taken away from our people, never to be seen, ever.

This woman was, of course, still Aboriginal by descent but by the age of 30 she was no longer *culturally* Aboriginal. Like thousands of others, she found it difficult to return to her people because she had only a vague idea where they were, because she knew nothing about them, because she was frightened of them rejecting her when she did find them, because she had come to be ashamed of her own Aboriginality and lastly because she had become scared of the very concept 'Aboriginal'. It was only later that she found out that none of this was accidental. *The people who had raised her had wanted this to happen.*

Why are the former State Wards so special, considering there are so many serious problems facing Aborigines today?

Partly, it is for those of us who remain with our families and communities. We need you and your children. More importantly, it is for you who had experiences that the rest of us can scarcely imagine:

> I've seen one Aboriginal girl flogged in that place and she could not walk, may God help me but she could not walk and after they had finished flogging her with a strap they would put her to bed and I never saw that Aboriginal girl ever again and she was only in there for a week and she was as black as black could be, a full-blooded Aboriginal girl and they used to call her Katie. And she got a hiding because she was screaming that she wanted to go home to her mother. And we asked her when she come in there how they got her in there and she told us that they took her out of her buggy and they

took her away from her mother away from the buggy and she said my father was in the bush because she said he was too frightened to come out because she said the policeman was after her father. And the mother was in the buggy with the baby and she said they took her and that she'd never ever, probably never ever see her mother. But she screamed for nearly two days crying to go home but they flogged her in the room and she was in the bed, like up in the dormitory where we were and she had marks on that girl's leg that were unbelievable, I never ever seen that girl after that, wherever she went to I don't know. However they got her out of bed to a hospital and covered it up. I don't know, but her leg was marked and some blood was coming out of the bruise on her leg.

What about the people who don't even know they are Aboriginal?

There are a surprising number of people of Aboriginal descent, even some who look recognisably Aboriginal, who have grown up believing that they are of European or Asian descent. Sometimes the substitute parents themselves believed it, for hospitals practised this kind of deception too. To discover suddenly that one is Aboriginal can come as a real shock. One of the people Link-Up has worked with found out that she was Aboriginal only when, at the age of nineteen, she wrote to the hospital where she was born. She received the news that her mother was Aboriginal in the 'non-identifying information' which hospitals and adoption agencies used to reveal. Another person, who had been sometimes mistaken for an Italian, began to wonder if she was really Koori after watching *Women of the Sun*.[2] Then partly by chance she met another Koori who knew her natural mother. So this question is not as silly as it sounds. There probably are hundreds of men and women in the state who don't even know, but may suspect, that they are Aboriginal, but who nevertheless want to know.

But my white friends say, 'How come you are suddenly Aboriginal when you've been white all your life?'

There are good, valid answers like 'It doesn't matter what colour your skin is', and 'I'm Aboriginal because I *feel* Aboriginal', but the answers probably won't satisfy your friends who, if they admitted it, may feel uncomfortable and maybe even a bit jealous. One answer you could give, which builds on the distinction we have already made between being Aboriginal by descent and Aboriginal by culture, would go something like this: 'Look, Aborigines are Aboriginal in two ways, by birth and by culture. I'm Aboriginal by birth but there is still a lot that I have to learn about the Aboriginal way of looking at life. Aboriginal culture is very different from white, even in New South Wales, though most white people don't realise this. There are different ways of relating to other people, for instance, or raising children, or settling disputes. I want to be a part of an Aboriginal community, be part of its history, and grow with it. I want to *culturally* become Aboriginal, and the best way to do this is to get to know my family.'

But my foster parents say, 'If we tell you who your real family is, you'll go off to them and we'll never see you again'.

If your relationship with your substitute parents is bad, that may well be true, but you probably would have separated from them in any case. But if you have a strong, mutually valuable relationship, it won't happen. If there is love and respect between you and your white parents—and there is no reason why there shouldn't be—you'll keep that relationship. Your Aboriginal family won't drag you away. Once they understand that you have a separate life somewhere else, they will be quite happy for you to live within those two separate sets of relationships. If your white parents are worried, you could explain to them that finding your natural family is a bit like getting married: they can only gain from your happiness in a new-found identity.

Haven't I still the right to go on living as a white person if I want to?

Of course you have. Link-Up will be happy to find

the relatives of any Aboriginal former State Ward, if that's what is wanted. If you then want to identify culturally as an Aborigine as well, we'll do everything possible to help you do that. It's your choice. From the point of view of the family too, we believe that the natural relatives have a right to communicate, only once if necessary, with missing family members. Say for instance that an aunt is looking for her niece. Link-Up believes that that auntie has the right to let her niece know that she loves her and wants to meet her. Link-Up undertakes to find the niece and pass on the message, if that's what is wanted. If then her niece chooses to ignore the message, that's her prerogative. Link-Up can do, and should do, no more. But this right of the relatives to make that first contact is an important once, especially considering the terrible experiences that so many of the former wards have been through, and the efforts of the whites to keep them away from other Aborigines. No one has the right, in our view, to stand in the way of a message getting through from the family to a mature adult. No one has the right to say (as Link-Up has sometimes been told), 'I know where he is but I won't tell you because it would only upset him'. People must be allowed to make their own decision.

What happens after I get in touch with Link-Up?

There is no one way in which Link-Up proceeds, because every request for assistance is different. Normally after a letter or phone call we'll contact you directly to arrange a meeting. In the course of this we'll talk about the different ways there are of finding missing people and what your options are. It could be that you aren't sure yet what exactly you want. If that's the case, you won't be hassled for a definite answer. It's your family, your experiences, your desires and your life.

What happens if I just want to find out who my relatives are, but don't want to meet them yet?

The choice is yours. We'll reassure you that there is nothing strange about this and that Link-Up exists to meet all the different needs that people have. We understand what you're going through.

I already know who my relatives are—is Link-Up any use to me?

We could be. If you are a former State Ward (instead of being fostered unofficially or through a religious adoption agency) your records may well be held in the State Archives of New South Wales. This is where the old government records are kept, in a building near Circular Quay in Sydney. Link-Up has the permission of the Ministry of Aboriginal Affairs (New South Wales) to seek information contained in the files of the former State Wards. Everyone, in fact, has the right to seek the Ministry's permission to look at the files of the former Aborigines Protection Board and Aborigines Welfare Board. However, like the Ministry, we are very watchful of privacy. Most people find that reading their own files is a mind-blowing experience. There will be many reports by welfare officers or institution officials that may be accurate or inaccurate, truthful or lies. There may be letters from your own mother asking for your return, or photos of you as a baby, sent by your foster parents to your natural parents, but which were never sent by the Board. There may be letters written by you, many years ago, whose existence you had forgotten. Therefore while we will willingly make a copy for the person who is the subject of the file, we won't do it for anyone else unless there are special circumstances. These might be, for example, where a file was requested by a child of a former ward who had died. But if, say, someone wanted to write the history of life in the homes and wanted to read some of the files, Link-Up would need the permission of everyone concerned.

Despite this, Link-Up has been able to get information from the files on 40 or 50 former wards who in every case have been fascinated (though often saddened) by what they read.

Link-Up can therefore provide information, or simply act as a sounding board, for people who want to talk about their experiences.

So I want to find my family. What now?

The search for a missing family can be very long—or very short. Our record for locating a missing family is two hours, but sometimes the search can go on for years. If we know the area your family comes from, the search can be fairly straightforward, although so many camps and reserves have been bulldozed or closed in the last 30 years that it's not uncommon to locate a family hundreds of kilometres from where the children were taken. Sometimes we know a surname but no place, which means that everywhere in the state where the family name is known has to be checked. In a few cases, mainly involving people over 50, we don't have knowledge of the family name or the area. These cases can be very difficult indeed.

The most useful of the old records held in the Archives are the *Register of Aboriginal Wards 1916–1928*, and the files of the former State Wards 1935–69.

The Register contains the names and brief case histories of 800 people removed in the period 1916–28. They list the family, birthplace and early history of each ward, making them essential reading for people in their sixties and seventies who still want to know who they really are.

In several cases we have tracked enquiries from families through the Register about wards who did not return home, only to find at the end something like 'Died Tuberculosis, Sydney 1927'. Our reply to the family will be the first message that the relatives have received since the day the ward was removed 60 years ago!

Most difficult of all are people in their seventies born too early to be included in the Register. One woman for whom Link-Up is working at the moment wants to find her true identity: all she knows is the orphanage she was raised in—no name, birthdate, birthplace or family.[1]

The files of the former State Wards 1935–69 are much fuller, especially for those children who went to the Aboriginal homes. The records for foster children are sometimes less complete, and for adopted children there are generally no records at all, for adoptions were handled through the Department of Child Welfare instead of the Board. However, as a preliminary to beginning to look for a missing person, we will check all the available records that are open to us.

When a family is looking for a lost child the search can be much more difficult. The old files will probably reveal no more than a last known address, and this might be 30 years old. There is no information to be had through the Koori network (the local 'grapevine' which will tell you the whereabouts of any Koori in town) for if the person we are looking for was identifying as Aboriginal, there would be no reason for the search in the first place. People in substitute care often have their Christian names as well as their surnames changed. To start the search with only the natural family name is to start a very long way back indeed, but that is where we have to start.

Other records that we may call upon are those held by the Adoptions Branch of the Department of Youth and Community Services, although by law any information relating to adoptions cannot contain anything from the original court records. The records of hospitals where many Koori children were born—Bethesda, Crown Street, the Mater and South Sydney—are often very useful. Public records that we also use regularly are the electoral rolls and the telephone books, though these have obvious limitations.

What if Link-Up can't find the person I'm looking for?

While it's true that Link-Up never gives up looking for a person, in urgent cases we concentrate all our efforts for a week or two on one particular case. Basically, given time, anyone can be found. Yet the length of time it takes to find one or two people is not just because of the large number of requests that we receive. The sources of information have to be streamlined too. So far we have put the two main collections of State Ward records held in the Archives into alphabetical order, which saves weeks of searching. In time we hope to gain access to the large number of foster files held by the Department of Youth and Community Services which probably contain as much information as those which we already have access to.

What's it like when you hear that your family is looking for you?

This is how John first heard the news:

> I often used to ask my foster parents about [my real parents] and they never told me much. All I knew was that I was born in Condo and my real name was Johnson. When I joined the Army I had to get on to my real name. Then I stuck to it.
>
> [Q]: *Do you think you would have ever gone home by yourself?*
>
> To tell you the truth, I probably would have still been wondering about it. See I didn't really know how to get in contact, and even if I did go back I probably would've bumped into them in the street, I wouldn't have known them.
>
> [Q]: *How did you know we were looking for you?*
>
> Yeah, it was quite funny. I was on my way back from the bank and one of me mates was passing in his car and said, 'Hey Johnno!' 'Yeah, right' 'Did you find out?' 'What?' 'Oh, your sister's looking for you'. I was scratching me head, 'cause I didn't really know I had one. And he says, 'Yeah, people have been up at the Castle [a pub]. They're asking about you'. I was living in another place in town, he knew where it was, and he said, 'Oh, yeah, I'll bring 'em round'. That day I went up there [the Castle] to find out who, and I went down to another pub, and they all said the same.
>
> [Q]: *What was going through your mind then?*
>
> Yeah, the message I got was 'your father loves you and he wants you to come home'. So I was sitting in the

91

pub, having a few beers, going right through me head, trying to figure out who the hell and what the hell was going to happen. I was rapt, 'cause I'd always thought about it, I knew where I lived and all that, Condo. I'd always thought about trying to find out who my real parents were, and the opportunity came to me and I said, 'yeah, I'll take it'.

[Q]: As we got nearer Condo what were you feeling like? Full of butterflies. I just didn't know what to say or what to do. And when I got there it worked out really well. Dad was really happy to see me and I was really happy to see him. Everything turned out really well. I didn't know I had that many cousins . . . My dad was really proud.

The first trip home

For John, as for almost everyone else who has found their family through Link-Up, that first day was the start of one of the most emotionally draining weeks of his life. Another person described it as 'having to re-live your whole life in a week'. So much that you've spent thinking—or agonising—about is suddenly made clear. The story of how you came to be removed, of brothers and sisters you've never heard of, of the local history of your own community, can come tumbling over you in such a bewildering fashion so that after almost every sentence you'll feel like saying, 'Stop for a minute and let me take all that in'.

Normally, Link-Up will have sent a telegram or

in some way have let your people know what time we expect to arrive. From the moment we start on the journey home, Link-Up is at your disposal. There will be one or two things that it will be useful to understand before you arrive. First, forget for a week or two about coming to terms with your Aboriginality—all that can come later. The only thing that matters at present is getting to know your people. Another thing we'll urge you do is to meet your people, but not to judge the house, the garden, the car or the town. Forget about material conditions for the present. For instance, you may be puzzled that your auntie lives in a house with broken windows on the reserve while her children have new houses in town—it's only later that you'll learn that she decided to remain as a statement of Aboriginality, or because the only town house available was next door to someone she disagreed with. It will take weeks or months before you begin to understand the history of race relations in the town, to know what has been possible for Aborigines to achieve there and what hasn't. Perhaps most important, don't ask too many questions. No matter how impatient you feel, it's best to wait to be told. For your family too you will be a stranger. You'll have to win their confidence by showing you are a fit person to receive the information. It may be years, literally, before you know the full story of your family's history.

A few miles out of town you'll probably want to stop, turn the car around and go home. But we'll go on until the car stops outside your house. Your people are inside. It's your family.

For the next few days, anything can happen and probably will. The best moments will be hearing 'g'day cousin' from dozens of different people, sitting up all night just talking, poring over the photo albums, sitting at your auntie's feet listening to stories of the old days, standing in a family photo for the first time in your life. The sad times will be hearing about relatives who worried about you all their lives but died too soon to meet you, or the trip to the very spot from which you were taken. You may feel awkward or tongue-tied, embarrassed because you can't put a name to the person you've already been introduced to three times. Then suddenly you'll feel strangely detached and find yourself asking, 'who are all these people? They are strangers to me'.

Link-Up can't promise that everything will be like this, nor that even at the end of a week, you'll think the whole thing worthwhile. Aboriginal families suffer the same number of life crises over two or three decades as anyone else, and on top of that there are the added strains of living as a repressed minority in a country town, or for long years under the yoke of some tyrant of a manager. It could be that your arrival revives memories of some old argument that you'll get caught up in even though it has nothing to do with you. And for you, there may be bad memories that you have to come to terms with. Feelings of resentment at your treatment or a lingering hurt at having been 'signed away'—all these things can take the edge off your joy at finding your real identity. There are so many conflicting emotions working inside you that when you look back on those first few days they will seem no more than a blur.

What Link-Up can promise you is that we'll be there when you need us. You may want to retire to a motel for a night or two, watch TV, talk all night or keep to yourself. We'll reassure you that these feelings are what everyone goes through. It has taken a great deal of courage to do what you have done.

Then, at the end of the week, if you want to stay, we'll push off. If you want to go back to your white friends and family, we'll take you. In fact most people are ready to go back at this point. The first curiosity is satisfied and you need time to think. You make the last farewells, shoot off another half-dozen photos and arrange to come back again.

Now what?

If it is true that the hardest thing you'll ever have to do in life is to meet your family, it's probably true that the second hardest is to do it a second time. After you get home it may occur to you that curiosity about what your family was really like had been one of your driving emotions, and now this is satisfied. You may feel unsure of your emotions: you know how you ought to feel towards your brothers and sisters, but somehow you still see them as total strangers. A woman who found her mother after more than twenty years, put it this way:

For five months after my return to Sydney I did not get in contact with my mother. I started to get depressed again. I had a quick burn out level. Then one day I asked why I was doing this to myself. I was only causing myself unnecessary pain. I then realised that, unconsciously, I had been testing my mother. I thought if she rang me, sounding worried, then that must mean she loved me. Stupid, stupid, stupid. I could have kicked myself as it began to dawn on me that maybe she thought I did not love her and that I wanted to break all ties. I had to remind myself that I was not the only one going through this experience. Mum was too. I rang her and she sounded so relieved to hear from me. She had been worried about me, but had not rang because she feared my rejection. She is trying to work through this experience as much as I am. She has the same doubts and uncertainties. She suffered the same gaping hole in her life as I did. She never received my love as I never received hers.

It's up to you and your family now to decide how often you'll write or phone, when you'll visit, whether you'll spend your holidays or Christmas there, or go to live there altogether. But, whatever you decide, it's unlikely that your Koori family will put any pressure on you, they'll just be happy to see you when you come. Even if you don't go back for a year they will be thinking of you constantly the way that they have always done. And when you turn up again, unannounced, someone will simply say, 'Oh, g'day. Good to see you'.

Is everything sorted out now?

Probably not. Almost everyone who meets their family for the first time as an adult takes months or years to feel confident in their new identity. For some people, especially those separated for more than 30 years, the gap is too wide ever to be bridged completely. We can't and we don't promise you the world. What we do promise is to help you fulfil as much as it is possible for you to achieve in your new relationship. And there will be some very real achievements. First the sense of not having identity, of not being the 'real you' will be gone. The mystery of the past is unrolled. No longer are you an Aboriginal in some vague generalised way, but an Aboriginal anchored to a particular time, place, family, community and history. When other Kooris ask, 'Who are your people?' you'll have an answer. Your family will have something solid too. No longer will you be the baby dimly remembered, a photograph in the Board's magazine *Dawn*, a name on the family tree. But above all, real achievements take time. The first week back is just a beginning. It takes time to be known and trusted. Then just when you are despairing of achieving what you'd hoped, there'll be a phone call to say that your father is going to call on you this weekend. During the writing of this booklet, two people whom Link-Up has worked with received phone calls like this, after eighteen months in one case and two years in the other.

Though I love my family, I still feel a little awkward and don't visit them as often as maybe I should. Am I still an Aboriginal?

Of course you are. First of all, you may find that instead of achieving a close relationship with all your family, you'll feel close to one or two people, a grandmother who remembers the day you were taken, a brother adopted out like you. Second, there is no one 'Aboriginal' view on anything, any more than there is any one kind of Aboriginal. This is what Link-Up is finally about: to help you achieve the maximum of what you want to achieve, both in terms of your family and your Aboriginality. Perhaps you'll never be able to call your natural mother 'mum'—but that's not your fault, it's the fault of the genocidal system which denied you your heritage and culture. You are not the less Aboriginal for that. You may find, with your new found confidence, that you want to work with an Aboriginal organisation. Go ahead. Your skills and experience are needed.

What happens when everyone has found their families?

Unfortunately, we can't see that happening in our lifetime. Many Kooris will die never having found their true identity, nor where their parents lie buried. The problem of removed children didn't end in 1969 when the Aborigines Welfare Board was abolished.

Aboriginal children are still being removed from their families every day, though under different laws. The Cootamundra and Kinchela homes are gone, but the children still are taken. Today 16 per cent of all children in government institutions are Aboriginal whereas the figure according to population proportion should be less than 2.5 per cent. Many of today's children in care still have no contact with their families. Some still don't even know they are Aboriginal, nor do their parents know where they are. These children will need help when they reach their twenties and thirties just as surely as those today who are in their fifties or sixties.

What can other Kooris do to help?

First, be understanding. Don't turn your back on Kooris in pubs who seem to stand there awkwardly or who have never heard of the Medical Service. Be sympathetic to those who don't say anything or go home early. Don't call them 'coconuts' because they aren't going to the football knockout. They may well be people separated from their families who are now trying to learn how to behave. It's hard to describe just how difficult it is for someone raised by whites simply to stand in a group of other Kooris. They need all the understanding, sympathy and love we can give them.

Link-Up also needs a network of support. In a few towns already there are people who have volunteered to act as local Link-Up agents. They are prepared to either take people home to meet their families if they live close by, or simply visit them if they want to get to meet some more Kooris. Link-Up needs your help as the movement back to family and culture gains momentum: it's growing every day. If you think you can offer some help of this kind, please let us know.

A last message to people who are thinking of taking the plunge

Reading books by anthropologists about Aboriginal life can only take you so far. The only way to begin to recapture your Aboriginal identity is to begin to live it.

Take your time. Don't move until you think you are ready, and please don't think that by contacting Link-Up that you are committing yourself to any particular course of action. When you think you are ready, make your move. It may be the beginning of a great adventure that will last the rest of your life. Physically, emotionally and spiritually your Aboriginality as well as your family are holding out their hands to say—WELCOME HOME!

1,2 Link-Up reunions. *Above*: Beryl Johnson and her father, Sibby Johnson, *c*. 1983. *Below*: Paul Cremen and family, 1985.

3 Wellington Valley, where some of the first stolen generations were seized in 1836.

4 Brungle Station, c. 1890. More than half the children were taken from here to Warangesda and, by 1920, many parents had left as well to avoid their remaining families being broken up.

The "Lutanda" Children's Home
WENTWORTH FALLS, N.S.W.

APPLICATION FOR ADMISSION

Date of Application........................... Date Admitted...........................

Name of Child *EILEEN WILLIAMS*

Date of Birth *13/9/1942* Place of Birth *.......Crown Street Hospital.......*

Name of Mother *Doreen Williams* If alive *Yes*

Name of Father........................... If alive...........................

Name of Guardian *ABORIGINES WELFARE BOARD*

Address and 'Phone Number *BRIDGE ST. SYDNEY*

Religion *PROTESTANT*

Why Admission is sought *TO TAKE THE CHILD FROM ASSOCIATION OF ABORIGINES AS SHE IS A FAIR-SKINNED CHILD*

Is applicant able to contribute towards cost of Support?...........................

....

A Doctor's Certificate MUST be obtained before Child is admitted.

Signature of Applicant X *Doretta Williams*

5 Joy (Eileen) Williams' committal notice, 1942. (*Courtesy of Joy Williams*)
6 The Bomadery Infants Home, c.1946. Joy is standing beside Sister Leila
Savile. (*Courtesy of Joy Williams*)

9 An Aborignal domestic servant in Sydney, wearing clothes similar to those Jane King would have worn

7 Joy, November 1948.
(Courtesy of Joy Williams)

8 At Lutanda, 1950. Joy is holding the doll, second from the right in the front row. *(Courtesy of Joy Williams)*

10 The Cootamundra Girls Home, c. 1930. (*Courtesy of the State Archives of New South Wales*)

11 The Kinchela Boys Home, c. 1950. (*Courtesy of the State Archives of New South Wales*)

12 The remains of Hollywood Reserve, Yass. The intention to clear this reserve to 'assimilate' the residents was used to threaten a mother with neglect of her children—unless she was moved to another reserve.

5

'I don't mix with Aboriginals, you know' Working with Link-Up clients

With the help of Nugget Coombs, Coral Edwards and I set up an office in the Australian National University recently vacated by the Aboriginal Treaty Committee. Coral was the co-ordinator, I was the co-worker.

Requests multiplied wherever we worked, as people heard of a way in which they might find their relatives separated long ago. A request to find John, mentioned in Chapter 4, followed our taking home his cousin Mary. These reunions were very moving occasions: Mary described meeting her family was 'like being born all over again'. But without the understanding that children had been taken as a matter of state policy rather than because their parents had neglected them, funding and bureaucratic support was difficult to find. Not even the Aboriginal communities seemed aware of why or how so many of their children had been removed, nor how they had been transformed into feeling ashamed of their Aboriginality. Removal in 1983 was still almost unmentionable by any family member involved. It seemed to reflect equally badly on one's family and oneself.

It was difficult also to explain to a client that parental homelessness generally was no accident. The parents of Jane King, for example, gave their six-year-old daughter to the Aborigines Protection Board—not because they did not want her but because they had nowhere to live. Jane King's one page official record notes the reason: 'No home nor likelihood of the same'. Why no home? Not because her parents were cheeky or lazy but because, at a stroke of a pen, the New South Wales Parliament had declared that they were no longer Aboriginal and therefore must leave their home on the Aboriginal reserve.

And now here 62 years later, at the other end of life, was that same child they had been forced to hand to the state: a grown woman who after twenty years in a mental hospital still spoke like a child, cleaned the streets of Sydney on her knees and refused to identify as Aboriginal. She had spent too long away from the firelight ever to wish to regain its warmth.

The experience taught me much about what might and might not be possible for families to achieve when they met after a lifetime apart. The following articles, then, are stories about two Link-Up clients, Jane King and Dianne Westmacott, whom I was privileged to work with both as historian and counsellor.

Jane King cleaning up[1]

I discovered the story of Jane King in the State Archives. The subject of one large file seemed to be the aunt of a young

Koori, Peter, whom I knew in Canberra, and I asked him what he knew of her. He had never heard of her, but his older relatives confirmed that his Aunt Jane had vanished from the family's knowledge in the 1920s and had not been heard of since. Peter asked Link-Up to find her, and it seemed possible that Jane's Archives file, which carried her story to the 1960s, might enable us to do so. After several weeks searching we located her in the inner Sydney suburb of Enmore. But it was all far too late.

Jane King (her name is fictitious) was born at Brungle on 12 March 1917. On 21 January 1921 her father, who had been living on the station for several years, fell victim to the 1918 amendment. He was adjudged to be 'an idle young half-caste' who ought to be earning a living off the station. The Board had no plans for his future beyond getting him off the station, so Robert King now had to do what others at Warangesda, Yass and Brungle had been doing for years: he made his way into the white community, picking up accommodation and employment wherever he could.

In competition with a recently demobilised white labour force, the chances of finding either may not have been great, but whatever hardships the Kings suffered is unknown. Probably in June 1923 they fell in with a welfare officer who told them that if they did not give over their child to the Board she would be taken anyway, and for a longer period. Perhaps they were told that she would have a better chance in the Homes, or perhaps the family was starving. According to the *Register of Wards*, Robert and Mary King arrived at the Cootamundra Home to hand their daughter Joan to the care of the Board. Joan was now six years of age. Her committal notice remarks coolly that Joan had been living with 'parents who wander about the country, having no home or likelihood of same'. They may have been told that they could have her back if they found a home, but whatever their expectations, they could not have realised that they would never see their daughter again.

Life at Cootamundra was bleak and sterile. The mental anguish of a sudden transition from family and community to an institutional life which reiterated daily the worthlessness of blacks was a burden which some found impossible to bear. One girl a little younger than Joan woke one night screaming and screaming. The next she had gone, where, the girls never knew. (We later discovered that she had been removed to a mental hospital where she remained for the rest of her life.) Of Joan's private world nothing is known beyond that her name was changed to Jane because there were too many Joans in the Home. Her daily lessons were washing, scrubbing and cleaning. Aboriginal girls had to prepare themselves for the day when they would be allowed to clean the houses of white people. Cleanliness was salvation, purging the worthlessness of a black body.

When Jane was just fourteen and separated from her Aboriginal culture for more than half her life, she was sent to her first domestic position at Centennial Park, Sydney, where her performance was described by the Homefinder as 'unsatisfactory'. In January 1932 she was transferred to another suburb where this time she was 'unsuitable and disobedient'. Next came a six-month stay with a woman in Gordon, followed by a further six months with another. At this point, when she was only sixteen, Jane's career as recorded in the *Register of Wards* ended abruptly. The Board had finished with her. However, most unusually, Jane's later life has been partly preserved in other written records.

In 1934 Jane entered the service of a Mrs Kingsley-Strack, a resourceful and outspoken critic of the Board. Here she remained for six years. In March, she sought the professional services of a Dr Kinsella. Early in 1939 the visits stopped, but in October 1939 she began to make threatening calls to his home. Kinsella alleged that on 17 February 1940 she phoned him eighteen times in three hours, in one of which she had said 'You are a dirty low-down dog, a murderer who operates when he's drunk, and killed a woman in hospital. You will get shot, you had better keep your children inside.' On the night of 22 November she threw a rock onto the Kinsellas' roof and ran off. The next night when she repeated the act Kinsella ran out to catch her. Jane alleged that Kinsella grabbed her by the neck and dragged her along the street. She sued him for assault.

At the hearing no evidence was entered as to how Jane had become a State Ward, nor what were the possible effects of institutionalisation at the age of six, nor the consequences of making a child ashamed of one culture without a welcome in the other. Nor was there any consideration of what might have taken place between Jane and Dr Kinsella so to aggravate her, though it appeared that Jane was not solely to blame. Mrs Kingsley-Strack claimed that Kinsella had once visited her home, seized Jane and cried 'You will be dead before nightfall'. The magistrate's verdict was fair: Jane's case was found proved but dismissed with costs. Little more than a year later Jane was committed to Parramatta Mental Hospital where several other women were also suffering from the consequences of being born Aboriginal in New South Wales after 1915. There she remained for 22 years.

In 1961 Jane wrote to the Superintendent of the Aborigines Welfare Board (as it had become known in 1941) identifying herself as 'a girl from the Abo board'. It appeared that the hospital regarded her as normal and wanted to discharge her. She had heard that new houses were being offered to Aborigines and wanted to know if she was eligible for one. How could Jane know that the new houses were not intended for ex-Cootamundra girls already wrenched from their community and culture, but were merely a bait to entice away the long-time residents of the remaining reserves? Jane's application was refused and in April 1962 she was discharged to a Catholic hostel where she earned her keep by selling raffle tickets. A social worker noted that no member of her family appeared to be 'actively interested in her'.

In 1981 Jane's nephew requested Link-Up to find her. We found her living by herself in a two-room flat in a Sydney suburb. She seemed to have few friends, and her greatest pleasure was to take day-return train trips to the country. When she did not have enough to do in the flat she would pick up the papers lying in the street outside her house and then clean up the area outside the local pub. Coral Edwards described how the first news of Jane's family was brought to her more than 50 years after her removal:

> She was mopping the hallway when I arrived, and I stood talking to her from the front door. She had difficulty following what I was saying about her family. All the time we were talking she kept mopping the floor. After about ten minutes, I said I was leaving and asked if I could take a couple of photos to show her nephew. She disappeared into the room to change her clothes. I sat on the front steps waiting. Fifteen minutes later she emerged. Dressed in her best outfit, blue frock, hat, stockings, high heels, carrying a hand-bag, she stood near the front gate for her photo. After taking a couple of shots of her, I asked if she would stand on the verandah. Through the camera lens I watched her step up to the verandah, pick up the broom that was standing against the wall, and sweep the doormat before standing on it. At that moment I saw her whole life history and all the conditioning that she'd been through, how deep it went. I broke down and cried.

Jane met her nephew several times in the next year, but was uninterested in meeting her younger sister. In 1984 all correspondence ceased. Coral wrote, 'She should have been an Aboriginal grandmother by now, surrounded by her family with all the warmth and love that goes with it. Instead she says, "I don't mix with Aboriginals, you know"'.

Throughout New South Wales there are hundreds of 'Janes', ashamed to the core of their Aboriginal heritage. Yet 'not mixing with Aboriginals' was entirely the point of the 1915 amendment. The cost was the well-being, and in some cases the sanity of thousands of Aboriginal children. The dozens of officials who had executed the separation policy so conscientiously might well ponder at this caricature of European civilisation who to this day cleans the streets of Sydney, on her knees, in answer to the obsession which has invaded her brain. Macrocosmic attempts at social engineering have a thousand microcosmic consequences which might well stay the hand of every reformer prepared to sacrifice the individual for the 'public good'.

The argument for the public good could in any case be upheld only if sufficient Aboriginal children ceased to identify as Aboriginal. Of the 70 Wiradjuri girls removed from their communities between 1916 and 1928, nearly one half fell pregnant in service, spent periods in mental hospitals or died. At the end of their training period, about half returned to their communities. A quarter did not return, or married white men, and there is no record of what happened to the others. Therefore, although many still suffer even today from their experiences, sufficient people did return to their communities to render the policy a failure. The destruction of women like Jane King was not only tragic but futile since the amendment foundered on the determination of those old enough to remember where they had come from to return home.

The two journeys of Dianne Westmacott[3]

Another early client of Link-Up was Dianne Westmacott, whose experiences before and after she met her family taught me much about the complexities of simultaneously trying to return to a lost family and to a lost Aboriginality. From working with Dianne I learnt not to be too ideologically starry-eyed, to help clients work within the parameters of what they wanted to happen instead of what I thought should happen. Dianne's story also demonstrates the enormous difficulties which adopted children faced in trying to trace their roots before the state Adoption Acts were changed.

Nobody knew for sure just who Dianne's parents were. They knew only that in July 1946 Mr and Mrs Westmacott had gone to Wagga for a couple of days and come back with a three-week-old baby. She had black hair and olive skin. To the cousins and rural workers of the property it was pretty clear that Dianne wasn't Anglo-Saxon. But what was she? Some speculated Negro; others maintained, in the local vernacular, that 'she had wog in her'. It was even whispered that it might be even worse: poor little Dianne might be 'dark'. Everyone had their theories—except Dianne. She didn't even know that she was adopted.

In the 1940s the New South Wales Department of Child Welfare gave no suggestions that substitute parents should tell their children that they were adopted.[3] Nevertheless it was an unusual adopted child that did not have a suspicion that there was something a little odd in its relations with its parents. So with Dianne. She wondered why her mother had not been discharged from the hospital at the same time as she, and why she was told always to pin her hair back 'because you look dark'. During a card game she heard her uncle say to the others that he hoped that Dianne's 'bad blood wouldn't come out' as she grew older. When she was about nine she overheard an aunt ask another aunt, 'Doesn't Dianne know who she is?' In response to her question Dianne was told, 'Don't you know? Your father was a Negro'. For an adult that would have been proof enough, but for a nine-year-old it caused only anxiety and confusion. What could it mean?

No one would elaborate and she was too frightened to inquire further. Nor did she realise the significance of other children seeing her as different. 'I was always being called black gin when I was a kid. I've always remembered fighting over me colour.'

When she was ten Dianne's mother became ill from a heart complaint. The family left the Parkes property and went to live in the Sydney suburb of Granville. Steadily Dianne's mother's condition worsened. She promised Dianne that one day she intended to return to Parkes to die: Dianne felt that she wanted, in her last days, to tell her something important. She was denied the chance. After a long illness Mrs Westmacott died leaving Dianne, now fourteen, in the care of her father, with whom she had never enjoyed good relations. Dianne recalled that after her mother's death she had heard stories of him telling people in Sydney that he was tired of living with an old crock. He told Dianne that if she had been sixteen, she would have been thrown out of the house. As it was, he said, she would have to stay home and look after him.

> [When mum died] my godmother came down from Parkes to get me, and said, 'I'll take her and bring her up' and all this, and Dad said, 'No, she's gotta stay and look after the house', and 'there'll be no one to look after me', and all this sorta garbage. But when Dad used to go to work I'd bring my friends in who were wagging school. He said I was uncontrollable and not looking after him properly. He went away to Parkes with this girl and I said, 'I'm coming too', and he

said, 'No, you're staying to look after the house'. I was fourteen and left in the house, and in them days they were real strict, and my next-door neighbour rang up the welfare and the welfare lady came and got me. He didn't even know I was charged. I was taken off Dad and charged with being neglected and exposed to moral danger.

It was at the magistrate's hearing, from which Dianne was released back into the care of her father, that she learned for the first time that she was adopted.

He tried to disown me in court and that's when it came up. The judge said, 'You cannot disown an adopted child'. [When we were outside] I said to Dad, 'I am adopted, am I?', and he said, 'Yeah, your mother's some bloody wog'. And I started getting a chip on the shoulder then. And I got uncontrollable. When I found out I was adopted I went around and terrorised Dad and threw rocks in his house and everything. I was a real bastard with a real big chip on me shoulder. And bashed up people and just got out of hand. I just was uncontrollable and hated Dad—it was just the way he said it and nothing I done suited him. You'd cook him a meal and he'd start picking at it or throw it out, and the floor wasn't polished good enough and he was bringing women home. Mum was only dead two weeks and he had a woman in the house and I asked him why he did it, he said, 'Well, if it's just thrown at you, you take it', and he was just a pig . . . In the end I got terrified of him and used to push cupboards up against the door. I started to get scared of him because of what the girls told me and that.

So Dianne was in court again, charged this time not with being neglected and exposed to moral danger, but with being an uncontrollable child.[4] She was ordered to the Parramatta

Girls Home. After three months she was transferred to a government hostel.

> In the meantime I'd been raped and when they found out I was pregnant they sent me down to Myee [another hostel] and I stayed there till Debbie was born. And then Mrs Donaghue [the mother of the rapist]—they were all rich—and she come down and said she wanted the daughter, it was the first granddaughter on the Donaghue side and all this garbage. And I was only fifteen and a half. They threatened me with [how] she could get it taken off me because she had the money, and even the Matron at Myee told me, 'Well you're better off letting that baby go, and letting it go to rich people.' And I said, 'No way. 'Cause this is my baby', 'cause I'd lost my mother and I was going to keep her. So she tried to get Debbie and she said, 'Well, we'll take you out to Cobar with us'. And when Colin got out of jail I married him to keep Debbie. Even the priest said it was a hypocritical marriage, that I was only marrying the father so that I could keep the child. They had this threat over me that I would lose her because I was under age, all this hogwash. And he was always coming home smashing you up, he was an alcoholic and I finally left him, and I haven't seen him now for 23 years.

Still Dianne was no nearer the truth about her origins, but it now appeared that her relatives had no better idea than her father exactly who her real parents were. Like him, they discouraged her efforts to find out. Dianne's uncle told her husband:

> If I told her about it, everyone'd get hurt, and if I told her, a mob of blokes'd go through your house and smash the house up, and you. They used to say to me, 'Look, we don't know what nationality you got in you, we just know your mum

111

came home to the property with you, that's all'. And I even used to think. 'What am I, a Mafia's daughter or something?'

False lead followed false lead. Dianne went to Broken Hill hoping to find someone who looked like her. At Walgett an old Koori heard her story and remarked that she probably had been stolen from his own tribe.

In about 1965 Dianne's husband Colin hired a private detective who somehow discovered that the name of her natural mother was Catherine Violet Gibson, nee Boys.[5] From her birth certificate (issued in her adopted name) Dianne knew that she had been born at the Wagga Base Hospital on 3 July 1946. With this information she visited the hospital to try to find out more about her family.

> I was 34 when I went to Wagga Base and said, 'I want to find out some information about my parents'. He didn't know I was adopted and he said, 'When was you born?'. I told him the dates and he said, 'Well we've had a flood and we mightn't even have the files', but lucky he found this big book. And he got intrigued and he started to tell the story [of a baby named as Gibson] and he said, 'It's a funny thing, there's only two babies born that day and you don't look like the Gibson baby to me because it was a little boy.' I said, 'Was there another baby?'. He said, 'You sure this was the hospital you were born in?' and I said, 'Yeah, it's on my birth certificate', and then he said, 'Well there's another little baby and her name is Boys, Caroline Boys.' He said, 'It must be you because this baby had "dark skin"' and all this. And she was put up in the nursery away from its mother and the other little baby went home with its mother . . . And then the superintendent of the hospital said he shouldn't have been telling me all this information because it was under the Welfare Act and all this. Then [despite this warning] I went to the Registrar's Office and it was only a young girl there

and I asked for my birth certificate under the name of Caroline Boys. She was going through this big book, and as she was looking I'd already seen everything before she got to it. It had stamped across it 'Under the Welfare Act' but she didn't notice. She was looking on this page and I was looking on that page, and I'd already seen it all. And then she looked and said, 'Oh, I'm not allowed to tell you nothing.' I said, 'It doesn't matter mate, because I've just seen it all.' And it had 'father unknown'.

Dianne's trip had, in a sense, been futile. She had already known her mother's name. The records did not specify any nationality. Why had her mother allowed her child to be described as 'dark' without giving further information? Who was her father? It seemed that records could help no longer. Only her mother could provide the information denied to Dianne for 35 years. Five years later the combined efforts of a firm of solicitors, the Adoptions Branch of the New South Wales Department of Youth and Community Services and Jigsaw, an organisation of adopted people, had failed to bring her any nearer to the whereabouts of her mother.

It was in March 1983 that Dianne phoned Link-Up. In the course of the conversation we asked why she thought that she might be Aboriginal. She replied that the Aboriginal counsellor at the school that her children attended had assured her, by her colouring and features, that she was.

The experience in Link-Up has been that most of the people who imagine, through hints by welfare officials or family members, that they may be Aboriginal, are in fact of Aboriginal descent. It was on this basis that we suggested that she write to the Adoptions Branch again to ascertain if all the information she knew about herself was correct. The reply, which closely followed the departmental guidelines about the release of 'non-identifying information' to adoptees, merely confirmed what Dianne already knew. She wrote to Link-Up:

> I got a letter from Youth and Community Services but I already know all the little parts they wrote me. They said her first names, not the surname, made out that's all they knew but you could tell they must have seen a file to give me what they said . . . The only thing I didn't know was that she lived, the last they heard, on the Riverina. So maybe if I look for her in the area. Her surname is Boys I think I told you anyway well thank you again . . .

Like the other agencies, Link-Up could make no progress in finding Dianne's natural mother until it had more biographical information. After several months we discovered that Catherine Violet Boys had been born in Melbourne. I wrote to Dianne:

> We learned this morning that mum, Violet Gibson (as she's known at Adoptions) and Violet Boys (as she's known at Births Deaths and Marriages) was born in Melbourne. If she was 26 at the time of your birth and you were born in 1946, that means that she was born in 1920.
>
> This means there is a chance that we might be able to get hold of her Birth Certificate, if you'd like us to do that. We haven't been able to find out much about your dad as yet, but that can come later if you'd like that. In the meantime, if you'd like to try for information about your mum, could you sign this form [requesting the Certificate] and we'll send it on to Melbourne . . .

The Certificate was returned to Link-Up. I wrote again to Dianne:

> . . . the important news is on your mother's side, we think. It says, as you'll see, that your mother's mother was Gladys Ann, nee— . . . . . , born at Echuca. Echuca is where the big Cumeroogunga mission station was (and still is) and

114

. . . . . . is one of the well-known families from there. We can't be certain yet, but it looks as though you could be related to the . . . . of Cumeroogunga . . .

Could you let us know what your feelings are now, and what you'd like us to do. Ring us up if you'd like to, and reverse the charges . . .

Dianne replied:

. . . Yes, could you go on with every thing you both have got a lot of information, that's for sure. I hope soon we will meet someone that knows my five brothers and sisters, seeing I was the 6th child.
P.S. Where is Cumeroogunga?
If my mother was alive she must be 65.

Diane Barwick was a person Link-Up often turned to when help was needed in tracing Victorian Aboriginal families. We wrote to her enclosing the birth certificate of Dianne's mother, asking if the information corresponded to any of the genealogies that she had compiled. She replied not with a letter but a parcel. It contained a copy of Scarlett Epstein and David Penny's *Opportunity and Response*,[6] which included her own history of Cumeroogunga.[7] There were photographs of family members, genealogies and a photocopied article about a distinguished forebear she had written for the *Australian Dictionary of National Biography*. With the package came a long excited letter explaining, in short, that it was time for Dianne Westmacott to come home.

She was related, it seemed, to two families who ultimately trace their ancestry to Old Maria, born in 1815, a member of the Wolligatha clan of the Pangerang tribe, whose language was known as Yotta Yotta or Yorta Yorta. What was more, her relatives would welcome her with open arms and loving hearts. 'Your client', wrote Barwick, 'would be welcome in the homes of any member of the Victorian Aboriginal community.' The letter ended with a moving paragraph. She did not, of course, intend that it should ever be published, but it stands nevertheless as a moving tribute to her contribution to the continuing cause of Aboriginal pride and self-identity:

> I hope this will be of some help. You and Coral [Edwards] are doing a job that William Cooper [the famous Victorian activist] would have approved: bringing home the children so cruelly taken away. He fought it all his life, and his kinsmen have continued on a national basis—to take pride in their Aboriginal ancestry and help others to understand the importance of the Aboriginal heritage. I am confident that your client will be gladly welcomed by a host of relatives if Link-Up can help him/her 'go home'. They have never stopped grieving for the children lost to their community.
>
> All good wishes, Diane

The first journey of Dianne Westmacott, to find her identity and her people, was almost at an end. She knew now that she was a direct descendant of a famous Victorian family who, through six generations, trace their ancestry to pre-invasion times.

Link-Up's next step, after consultation with Dianne Westmacott, was to travel to Melbourne. We learned the address of one of Dianne's oldest and closest relatives, her great-aunt, who lived in a Melbourne nursing home. Following our usual practice we proceeded cautiously at the meeting: no one could know in advance what old memories might be revived at the mention of Dianne, nor whether her birth had been known about at all. There was no problem. It turned out that Dianne's great-aunt was living at the time with her mother: she knew about the baby and how Dianne's adoption had been arranged. Photos were exchanged and in November 1984 I wrote to Dianne:

We have some good news for you, as we have just been to
Melbourne to find out some more about your family. After
asking about a bit, we went to see Mrs . . . . . . , who is
your great-aunt. She is a lovely old lady, about 77, who lives
in a nursing home in . . . . . ., Melbourne. She knew a lot
about your mum, and another sister . . . What's more, she'd
love to see you some time if you can get to Melbourne, and
is only sorry that she can't have you to stay, but being in
a nursing home, it's not possible.

So what we'll do now, as soon as possible, is go and see
your mum with your photo, and explain what's happened
so far. Then we'll get back to you and bring you up to date,
and if all goes well, we might be able to introduce you to
her . . .

There was plenty that might not go well, for the initial
contact with natural mothers (or children if it is the parents
who approach Link-Up) is the most difficult task of all.
Almost all natural mothers remarry. Frequently they do not
tell their husbands, or later children, about the adopted child.
No one can be contacted in advance to test the waters, for
neither the sisters nor closest friends of adopting mothers can
be assumed to know about the birth of an adopted child.
Link-Up's policy is to approach the natural mother at the
time when she is most likely to be alone, but if she is not,
to ensure that the conversation takes place in private.

It was at about 2.30 pm, in early December 1984, that
we approached Catherine Violet Anderson, nee Boys, at her
Sydney home to inquire about her adopted daughter. When
we asked for her by that name she guessed—like most adopting mothers—what we had come about. She came out onto
the veranda so her husband, watching television inside, could
not hear. Yes, she was Dianne's mother. Yes, she would like
to see her photograph. Yes, she would like to meet her, and
had been thinking about her a lot recently following some

publicity about adoptions in a magazine. But no, she had not told her husband nor any of her other four children about their adopted sister. The first meeting would have to be in secret, but, so as not to arouse the suspicions of her husband, it must be at a place where Catherine normally might be found. He and the children would be told after she had met Dianne.

Before the meeting we again visited Dianne to explain that the whole of a future relationship can depend on the first crucial few hours. It was good to take along a photo album, to talk about the children and the recent past, but not to dwell on childhood unless asked. Above all, we urged her to avoid, for her mother's sake, those vital questions that had gnawed at her for so long: why was she adopted, and who was her father? It was better to wait to be told without asking, though this might take hours, weeks, even years.

The meeting was to take place at a cafe at the Westfield Centre, Parramatta, at 11 am on 14 December. At 10.30 we picked up Mrs Anderson at the end of her street, as she had suggested, so her husband would not see the car. She waited in the cafe while we went to meet Dianne at Parramatta Station. We walked to the cafe, introduced them to each other, and left. A week later Dianne wrote to Link-Up:

> . . . Anyway all went well. I let her do the talking 11.30 right through to 4.30, boy I know where I get my talking from. We met again at my place the following Thursday, she gave me a jewel box she got me at eighteen years. She is a nice lady but I still feel just a friend I don't feel like her daughter but I guess that's natural. So she wants to meet a lot, but she is always telling me about the whole family all the time, she is wanting to meet my mob, she said she will try to come to Linda's 21st so she will meet the whole family my Linda looks a lot like her . . .

Many people are worried at first that they seem no more than friends to the parents they have just met for the first time. But for Dianne, the two years after they met brought no improvement. In 1987 she still felt outside the family circle. She had met few other relatives, her mother had still not acknowledged her publicly, she had not met her great-aunt, and her Aboriginality was regarded by her mother as something best forgotten.

[At the first meeting] she said she would've known me any-where in the street. We sat down and had a cup of tea. She said she went to Wagga looking for me when I was fifteen, 'cause she'd know me anywhere in the street, but she never found me. She always thought I was well looked after, but then she got onto her family. She keeps getting off 'em and onto her other [Anderson] family. And I didn't want to put too much on her at first, 'cause I might've frightened her away, and I just said, 'Where's my real father?' and she said he died of a heart attack and she explained she was with this other bloke.

[Q]: *Did she explain how you came to be adopted?*
She'd left the first two children with the grandmother and she went with this bloke and fell pregnant, and then the bloke turned out to be married from somewhere, so she said she wasn't getting rid of me until she was in the hospital and the matron said these people are wealthy and they can't have any kids and they would like to adopt the baby. She didn't sign the papers till five years later, but she let the matron take me up to the nursery and she never seen me again, she only seen me the first time. She couldn't drag me from pub to pub because she was cleaning pubs and stuff. And then she came down to Sydney and met Mr Anderson and she got married and had two other kids to him. She kept me a big secret. All the four are together, but nobody knew about me

119

. . . She didn't do too much talking about the past, she was talking about general life, she just kept jumping away from it all the time. Even now I've gotta ask her, and I still haven't asked her, why she called me Caroline. 'Cause she keeps getting off it, and she just doesn't seem to wanna talk about it.

[Q]: Did she know that you knew that you were Aboriginal?

Yes, I showed her the pictures of the ancestors that you gave me, and they're really black. She goes, 'Where did you get these from?' I said, 'Link-Up found them', and I showed her the articles and that. She took photocopies of them all 'cause she said, 'That's interesting, I might start tracking down a few of my relations.' That will help her—I don't think she knows many of her people. She told me she didn't know she was Aboriginal till she was nineteen.

[Q]: Have you ever met the two daughters she had to Mr Anderson?

No, she never ever says their surname or their addresses when she's talking about them, even though she's always talking about poor Shirley this and poor Shirley that . . . That dark guy Greg I was with [in 1986] said, 'I'd give her a big miss, 'cause if she was going to say anything, she'd be saying, "Why don't you come up to the club and I'll bring it out now?" It's a bit past a joke if you've gotta be sneaking round all the time.' And she didn't like him because he was black. I thought she might have had a bad experience with black people, but I don't know.

[Q]: How did she come to meet him?

I picked her up. She wanted to come to Linda's 21st, well Greg was living here, I was going with him for nine months. I said to her, 'I've just gotta fly down here and pick Greg up' . . . Soon as she seen him coming, she said, 'Oh, you're not going with him, are you?' I said, 'Yeah, that's my old man.' She said, 'No, I'd give him a big A', she said, 'because you'll

end up in hospital with a broken jaw or something,' she said
. . .

[In the end] I started to get a little bit mad with her,
because she's not bringing me out, not even slowly bringing
me out, you know, and I have asked her was she ashamed of
me, and I have asked her was she prejudiced. She reckons
she's not. But she's hiding me in the closet, it's nearly two
years . . . She's sorta going along like we're just friends, and
I don't feel anything. Sometimes I feel more angry 'cause she
not doing anything.

That's what was happening when I used to fight with me
step-dad. That was our twenty-year feud, because he wouldn't
tell me the truth. It built up inside me and I don't want it
to happen again 'cause I had a real big chip on my shoulder.
I start getting [the same feeling] when I'm with her.

Dianne's story, though in its way unique, is also typical
of those of many other adopted Aboriginal adults. It was, and
is, common for adopting parents to hide the facts of birth
and racial descent, sometimes out of some psychogenetic
fantasy that some day 'blood' will 'out'. Many parents do not
realise how desperately their children will want to know their
origins. Baffled by discrimination against their children in
school, they can offer no help beyond a reassurance of their
own love. Twenty years of good relationship between parent
and child can be ruined by the search for natural parents, the
real identity, but it is also not unusual for an adoption, as in
Dianne's case, to break down completely.

Though some reunions are spectacularly successful, many
do not follow the fantasies long rehearsed in the minds of
separated children. In the twenty, thirty or forty years between birth and reunion, parents remarry, or die. Families can
disintegrate. Young adults who want to begin to live as
Aborigines often find that the degree of Aboriginal identity

in their families (which can range from passionate involvement to off-hand denial), does not match their own expectations or desires. Though Dianne didn't particularly want further counselling, follow-up work can go on for years after a first meeting. Every six months Link-Up people meet together for a weekend of talk and relaxation. It is here that some find a new Aboriginal community, a second family, but even people who have formed good relationships with their natural kin-folk are strengthened by companionship with others in similar positions. They seem to be the only ones who really understand how difficult it is to begin living an Aboriginal identity after a lifetime on the other side. For, as all the people who have found their families through Link-Up know, the reunion is the end of one journey but the start of another.

So Dianne's second journey has begun. She now identifies as a Koori, and has cousins to stay. She has that satisfaction of being able to put a face on a natural parent that only those who are adopted know. Above all she has an answer to those questions which Kooris ask each other when introduced: 'What's your name?' 'Where are you from?' 'Who are your people?'

Like other adopted Aborigines, Dianne probably will not arrive at the goal that hovers seldom nearer than the far horizon: how to feel completely comfortable and secure within both the immediate and distant family circle. Even if, as is her present plan, she decides to contact her great-aunt, there are months or years of awkwardness, ignorance or anxiety. The loving hearts of the Victorian Kooris will need to be understanding as well as sympathetic. But it is the returning children who have to change the most. Dianne Westmacott stopped growing as an Aboriginal on the day she was adopted. On the day she met her mother she was 37 years younger, as an Aborigine, than her contemporaries who stayed behind in the communities. To find peace as an Aboriginal family member she has to put aside the fears, the attitudes, the memories, the ignorance; probably in modern Australian society there is no journey which requires greater courage of herself nor understanding of others.

Like hundreds of other people who in the last five years have set out in search of a family and an Aboriginal identity, Dianne Westmacott will find that each year will bring her closer to what she has been denied. There will be rewards on the way: flashes of insight, annual visits, people to stay, family secrets, a place in the albums, invitations to weddings and funerals, midnight-to-dawn conversations, unexpected phone calls, Koori stickers on the kids' suitcases. Unlike the first journey, the second journey never ends. But it is the journey, not the arrival, which matters.

6

At the edge of the firelight
Coming home, partly[1]

Apologists for the removal of Aboriginal children frequently cite the success of high achievers and exceptional individuals like Charles Perkins and Lowitja O'Donoghue as evidence that the practice was not only full of good intentions but achieved good outcomes for individuals. It is interesting to see how such individuals analyse their own stories and what conclusions they reach.

Here I pay particular attention to Charles Perkins. This is partly because I know him best, having written his biography, and partly because of his high intelligence and capacity not only for self-analysis but for seeing his personal situation in historic and political context. Charles' story is important for another reason. I said earlier that I had only gradually become aware of the full extent of the tragedy of the Stolen Generations, and my attitudes had gradually changed as I did so. This is also the case with many of the people who were separated and as they have aged their reflections on their lives have changed in complex ways. Part of the complexity is that while the children suffered traumas, in some cases they came into contact with loving and caring individuals who nurtured them and for whom they maintained a life-long respect and affection. While they might see the system as evil, individuals within it might be good.

In the case of Charles Perkins, we are in a very good position to see and partly understand the changing attitudes over time. Not only did he write his own story in 1975, but I began his biography, based in part on detailed interviews with him, fifteen years later; then he reviewed that manuscript with me in 1989. In what follows we see his changing attitudes to his experience over two decades.

Charles was separated from his mother and his Alice Springs Arrernte community at the age of nine. He was then raised in St Francis House, an institution in Adelaide.

I regret it bitterly

In 1945, at nine years old, Charles was leaving Alice Springs for the first time. His mother Hetti had agreed to allow Father Percy Smith to raise him, and five other boys, in a family home in Adelaide.

The six boys to leave Alice Springs in January 1945 were John Palmer, David Woodford, Malcolm Cooper, Peter Tilmouth, Bill Espie and Charles. There was a large crowd to see them off at the station and more of the boys' relatives gathered along the track for a kilometre or two to wave goodbye. There was more excitement than tears. To Charles it seemed a holiday rather than a new life; so great was his excitement that he cannot remember whether it was day or night. In fact it was day. A photograph was taken from the train: 50 people stand in groups, seemingly motionless and

silently a few minutes before departure. As the train moved
Charles had a last glimpse of the houses of Rainbow Town
as the Ghan pulled through the Gap.[2]

When they arrived it was evening on the third day. The
party spent the first night with a relative of the Smiths' in
the industrial seaside suburb of Semaphore. The boys rushed
down to the beach to discover the water was salty and the
land strange. Some time later the party moved to the converted eight-bed hospital in Kensington Park that had been
lent to Smith. Perkins found that the aura of its former
existence remained. It was too clinical, too clean for him to
be comfortable. But there was a shed to muck around in at
the back and the boys could go to school without opposition
from white parents. There was a big clock on the mantelpiece,
'ding donging all the bloody time'. Smith listened to the
clipped tones of the ABC newsreader: Perkins, who had never
heard a news broadcast before, wondered why a stranger was
reading to himself.[3]

Not long afterwards Gordon Briscoe arrived from
Balaklava and the following eighteen months were the closest
time the seven boys shared with the Smiths. Bill Espie
recalled Smith reading *Winnie the Pooh* round the fire each
night, ending with 'Okay boys, into bed'. Meal times were a
focal point. There was a high Anglican emphasis on decorum
and gentility. The table was set with a lace tablecloth, the
butter cut into cubes, there was bone china as well as crock-
ery, silverware instead of tin, cups and saucers instead of mugs.
Tea passing was something of a ritual. Mistakes were corrected
by Mrs Smith, 'My dear, you're not supposed to . . .' Today
many of the lads are neat and discreet eaters who still leave
a bit extra on the side of the plate. They wore suits, shoes,
underclothes, some for the first time. The house itself Briscoe
recalled as cluttered and wintry—leadlights, heavy curtains,
crochet work.[4]

The church underpinned daily life. In a converted room there was chapel twice a day. On Sunday the boys dressed up in their suits and went across for Holy Communion. Sometimes they went three times in a single day: 'You'd spend more time on your knees than you would standing up.' Some of the boys, as a consequence, they say, of too much church-going, have not attended a formal church service since leaving the home. Under all was the Smiths' warm love for their charges not only as participants in a 'remarkable and innovative act of faith' but as individuals treasured as if they were their own sons.[5]

Probably as much love was bestowed upon the boys by the Smiths as on any children in the long history of Aboriginal institutions. There was no paid staff. Percy and Isabel did all the work until Mrs Smith's cousin, known as Aunt Jingle, came to help. Money was tight even after the Commonwealth government provided a subsidy. On Saturdays Smith sometimes took the boys to football matches, or at night to the pictures. Out would come the pocket-money tin, kept replenished by parents back in Alice Springs. If anyone was short, the deficit would be made up by Smith himself. Sunday mornings were letters-home time, even if few parents could read or write. Each letter was filled with phrases suggested by the Smiths, like 'I hope you are well'. Sometimes on Sunday nights Smith took the boys to fellowship tea. The message to the parishioners was always that the 'half-caste' boys, given an equal chance, were their equals. After school there was homework, games, gathering pine cones in the park for the chip heater, formal tea, washing up, chapel, bath and the bedtime story. Mr and Mrs Smith seldom had any time for themselves.[6]

Charles was loved as much as the others. The Smiths seemed to have understood him well, and he responded to their warmth. He was lively and affectionate, sang in the choir, and did not answer back as Malcolm Cooper sometimes did. But he was more sensitive to slights than the others. He would fight on and on with other boys, sometimes past the point of good sense. If he had fought with a friend like Espie, he might nurse a private hurt for a week. He missed the relationship with his mother and, for all the Smiths' love, carried a private loneliness probably unperceived by the adults. The racist taunts cut deeper into his perceptions than those of the other boys.

Some incidents were amusing in retrospect. One night a crowd of boys ran towards the Aborigines shouting 'let's get the niggers'. The St Francis boys joined in the chase, until they realised that they were the ones pursued! But some of the insults burned and continued to burn, embedded in the memory, though their meaning eluded Perkins for some years. 'That's the way it was, we accepted it.' One member of the Anglican Church chased the boys away with 'I don't want you black kids hanging round'. Another, after a youth fellowship meeting, kept the boys on the veranda while the adults went inside.[7]

For as long as Smith received no subsidy from the government, his only wider concern was with his superior, the Bishop of Carpentaria. Smith remained under an obligation to him for allowing him to remain outside the diocese, an absence tolerated partly because the bishop viewed the experiment as a forerunner of more fundamental social engineering. By December 1946 the bishop had plans to move at least a further 50 part-Aboriginal boys from the Northern Territory to Adelaide, from where, he hoped, they would never return. Within the church there was some dissension at the plan, but every time Father Smith went north he came back with one or two boys, at his own request, or their mothers' or the bishop's. It was the price that had to be paid for his continuing absence from the parish. The result was that the

Pembroke Street home became rather too crowded for its intimate family atmosphere to continue.[8]

Some months later Smith spotted an imposing, though dilapidated, 26-room house near the beach at Semaphore. With some opposition within and without the church he raised a loan, bought the house and moved the home from Pembroke Street to Semaphore in August 1947. On moving day, Charlie Perkins, Bill Espie and Father Smith rode the 30 kilometres down to the port on a horse and dray. The institution became known as St Francis House and the boys of the home to this day are sometimes known as 'St Francis boys' or 'Father Smith's boys'. Eventually the older boys were awarded their primary education certificates. Malcolm Cooper and Charles Perkins had done best, so for a few months of the following year they put on their caps and suitcoats to travel by bus to Woodville High School. It was not a success: there was too little money, too little expectation that they would succeed, and the boys' educational level was too low. A year later Perkins and Cooper joined the others at Le Fevre Boys' Technical School across the paddocks from St Francis House.[9]

When Smith took his eleven boys to enrol them at Le Fevre, someone called out 'Look at that mob of damned blacks'. A fortnight later there were no taunts because the white boys were scared of the St Francis House lads. All were good fighters. The boys were sporting heroes for a day and won grudging respect for their prowess at athletics and Australian Rules, but there were no scholastic successes. No one expected the boys to do well, and no one was surprised when they did not. Perkins was told by a teacher that he did not have the brains to carry on after third year. Could the St Francis staff have taken an interest in their schoolwork? Could someone from Le Fevre have coached the lads after school? Perkins concedes that the questions are out of time: no one did that sort of thing then.[10]

Some time in 1946, with the arrival of the boys from Mulgoa hostel in Sydney, the character of St Francis House changed from that of a family style group-home to a small institution. They had left the Northern Territory in 1942; now, after some press controversy, the church had decided to close the Sydney institution. The girls went to Alice Springs and the boys to St Francis House. The new inmates included Wally McArthur, John Moriarty, Jim Foster, Gerry Hill, and Ken and Cyril Hampton. McArthur, older than the others and a fine athlete, became the leader of the St Francis House boys. Hill, who went from Alice Springs to Mulgoa in his mother's arms, had remained there after she died until the institution closed, and arrived at St Francis at the age of eleven. John Moriarty was born at Borroloola but had travelled with the others from Alice Springs to Mulgoa. At St Francis House he noticed at once the contrast between the clothes: in Sydney he had walked to school in bare feet. He and the other Mulgoa boys were conscious of being thought sissies for reading their bibles and never swearing; a sensitive, conscientious boy raised in the Low Church Sydney diocese, he remembers a few religious arguments with the High Anglican Smith. Soon after the Mulgoa group, another lad entered the circle of kinship, camaraderie and loneliness developing among the inmates of St Francis House. He was Vince Copley, small and dark, in a little grey suit and blue cap. He was eleven years old and born at Point Pearce mission, near Adelaide, although he had been placed from Alice Springs. His mother brought him to St Francis House. She waited for a couple of days before leaving him. For Vince the first six months were the worst, but once he stood up for himself, he was happy.[11]

Whatever his attitude to the boys' Aboriginality, Smith

encouraged family ties where he could. The annual highlight was the return to Alice Springs. On the train a grand time was had by all, except, possibly, Father Smith. There was no money for sleepers, so the boys lay down on the open section at each end of the carriages or roped each other into the luggage racks. At stops they would jump out and stockpile rocks to throw at empty bottles lying at the side of the track. As they approached the Alice, cousins and aunties would be standing and waving for a kilometre or two before the station. Then the boys would be mobbed and seldom spoke to white people until the end of January.[12]

There followed each year a few golden weeks. Espie remembers Hetti passing pies for Perkins, Moriarty and himself out the back window of Underdown's cafe. Moriarty, without a family in Alice Springs, spent many hours with Hetti. When Bill Espie went home, his mother watered the floor to settle the dust. The tang and the gentle steam rising from the red earth of his homeland under the midsummer sun is locked in Espie's memory forever. Meanwhile the old people were trying 'to cram a hell of a lot in' by making sure the boys did not waste any time mixing with the whites.

By this time Hetti had moved to a room out the back of Mrs Espie's house, where she and her children Charles, Ernie and May had only a bucket to wash in. Charlie and 'Coop' (Malcolm Cooper) sometimes went up to stay with Charlie's brother Bill Turner, the stockman at Alcoota who was not allowed to associate with the blacks.[13]

By the end of that first year the boys were not quite the same. Espie told his mother that she should use serviettes and everyone laughed. Charles tried to do the same:

> I can remember the greatest thing in my life [at St Francis House] was going to tell my mother when I returned, [I] was really going to show her how much I'd progressed. I was

going to cut butter into squares. That was really something I thought, that was my burning desire all year to tell her how that should be done. I have a real laugh about that now, when I think—God, you know, what a stupid thing. I thought, my mother is really backward, she's gotta know how to cut butter into squares. When I told her about that she nearly went through the roof. She was flat out getting butter let alone cutting it into squares! Everybody else laughed and I realised how ridiculous it was . . . I could see St Francis was pulling me away from Alice Springs.[14]

What did Mrs Espie and Mrs Perkins make of such antics? Espie wonders whether his mother came to regret the prolonged absence of her son. To Perkins the tragedy of separation was that for his mother the first farewell at Alice Springs Station had been also a last goodbye. She had known it but her Charlie had not. Adelaide was another country. For the younger boys, with fewer memories and a weaker grip on kin relationships, the separation was even more marked. Little by little the old people were slipping away. While at St Francis House, Gerry Hill had not missed the red earth, and now as the train pulled out at the end of the holidays he did not care that his aunties were worrying and crying for him. Gordon Briscoe didn't come back at all at the end of that first year. His mother was still at Balaklava, and he was nervous of returning to Alice Springs without her.[15]

Midway through 1948 the bishop asked Smith to return to Alice Springs to care for the parish to which he was nominally attached. It had, it appeared, declined under the charge of another priest. For Percy and Isabel Smith it was an agonising decision. In the end (perhaps they had no choice) they decided to return. In the recollection of all the boys, the atmosphere of love and understanding which had characterised St Francis House so far went with them.

First in everyone's memories following the Smiths' departure was a superintendent (he was no longer known as 'father') who sometimes beat the boys in the showers with a high-pressure hose. Another, a former soldier in New Guinea, insisted on the spit and polish standards of the armed services. A severe institutionalism replaced the pastoral care of the Smiths. Standard punishments included extra washing up and the deprivation of supper, pocket-money or the pictures. Gerry Hill recalled the boredom of weekends: after the Smiths went, nothing much was organised. On the weekends there was nothing to do but play on the sandhills and throw stones at the gangs of white boys. Espie recalls how on several occasions he and Perkins, in return for free board and lodging (which they received at St Francis House anyway), were farmed out to people who wanted some weekend labour. The two boys had to follow a dray about the Adelaide streets, scooping up manure for the garden of their temporary 'employer'. Always the boys were hungry. Espie and Perkins used to walk down the gutters of nearby streets to pick up thrown-away fruit. After twenty minutes they gathered round a bin, scraped out the bad bits and ate the rest. Perkins rummaged in bins in the hope of finding clothes and shoes better than his own. From the Alice, far away, Father Smith heard of these developments and regretted that he had left. He believed that it might have been better to have placed the boys, in ones and twos, as foster children in loving families. Having a group of dark boys together attracted the 'stares of the credulous' and got in the way, he believed, of assimilation.[16]

But the Australian Board of Missions congratulated itself on its achievements. Readers of the 1952 ABM *Review* were assured that the 23 boys rose at 6.15, made their beds, breakfasted at 7.00, did a few chores and went to school. Each evening the smaller boys played while the older lads did their homework; all were in bed by 10.00 unless special permission was granted to go visiting. The *Review* explained that the problem was that in 'spite of special pleading by isolated champions part-Aborigines were still treated as Aborigines by the laws governing the conduct of full-bloods'. The Northern Territory government was less impressed. In 1954 the Director of Native Affairs, though pleased that the institution was 'definitely accomplishing the objectives of assimilation' was also irritated that the board decided which children should go, sometimes taking boys who had parents or homes in Alice Springs in preference to 'more deserving cases in other parts of the Northern Territory'. He was also concerned that a single young man had sole charge of the boys.[17]

Perkins's relation to the staff following Smith's departure seems to have deteriorated more than the others'. He was a boy who responded quickly to both affection and dislike; he had formed a fast, close bond with Smith and now fell out almost as fast with Smith's successors. He became more aggressive to the staff and to whites in general. After a perceived injustice, the indignant 'Did you hear what he said then?' would be followed by a call to action. Perkins's particular memories include a superintendent's wife, 'a vicious bastard of a woman' who hated him, and of being punched in the guts if he wasn't standing straight at inspection. One morning:

> I went down the fire escape, my cousin and I, Laurie Bray.
> He told us to go up, back that way. We were on the way to
> school. We got upstairs, and we were coming down again,
> and he caught us down the bottom. Well he belted this
> Laurie, and I couldn't get out of the road. Then he got hold
> of me and he gave me such a whacking I couldn't get out.
> He knocked me down so I couldn't even stand up, he was
> bashing me until he broke the broom handle, he went mad,

a big stick like that and he smashed and broke it. Then he stopped and he had to go and sit down he was that exhausted. Well I couldn't move either. I was battered away there, and I crawled about 40 yards down to the bathroom and just lay there for about an hour. I was on me way to school, mind you. Got there late, got into trouble. And none of those blokes [teachers] had any idea of what we had to go through, to get there . . . Oh, they've got a lot to answer for, these bastards. And the worst part, they were priests. Anglican priests! I'll for ever have a hatred of Anglicans. I'll never let it go.[18]

In 1952, at the age of sixteen, Perkins was ordered to leave following yet another argument with another superintendent. Also there were difficulties with the older, apprenticed boys who demanded treatment different from the lads still at school. A scheme to open a second, cottage style group-home for the apprentices had come to nothing.[19] So out Perkins went with only a few days notice. He stood outside St Francis House, having known no home but the institution for six years, with nowhere to go and an injunction not to return. With a battered suitcase and worn-out shoes he looked like just another Adelaide Aborigine. Was this all there was to being given another name in another country? No. Though his possessions were few, Perkins now carried some of the essential baggage of the whites in his head.

To the home he had brought his own, still latent, family values of self help and entrepreneurial endeavour, but the years of institutionalisation had changed both his personality and worldview. At St Francis House Perkins learned toughness, discipline and an independence of spirit. Politeness, order in daily life, consideration in men, gentility in women were the outward manifestations of his social values. John Moriarty reflected:

[The] sense of decorum which we have which is very much the basis of our individual personalities. Charlie, when he gets dressed, he gets dressed well, and when he goes out he has a good time. We were very much structured. We were very much structured in the sense that we utilised all our time. We'd start off with church in the morning. Go to school, come home, we were part of the old school system establishment, particularly Anglican system. School clothes together, hung up in the wardrobe, dressing gown, (which we'd not had before). Our singlets and our play clothes and our school clothes. And our intermediate clothes. Our shoes would be polished every morning. There was that sense of compartmentalisation of our duties which meant that what you did at school, you had to do then. What you did after was part of your free expression after school. But you had to change to do it. Then you'd come to your meal, you had to wash and there'd be a certain type of food that you'd eat with certain manners and dignity. Everything was pervaded with that dignity. Then you'd have to go bed at a certain prescribed time, you'd have to have a bath, clean, pulled up on your manners and pulled up on your cleanliness, personal as well as general. The whole lot taught us to be very neat, methodical. Utilise the best of your time. The achievers in any society have done that.[20]

Gordon Briscoe also analysed the intellectual baggage of St Francis House. He noted the somewhat seminarian ambience of work and chapel, life with a purpose, bourgeois gentility combined with working-class job expectations. While the Aboriginal girls of the Colebrook Home a few suburbs away pursued professional or semi-skilled careers such as office work or nursing, Smith's horizon was the apprenticed trades. It may have been a vision more practical than limited. He may have believed that society would not accept Aborigines in the professions and the failure of Perkins and Cooper at Woodville High may have warned him not to set his sights too high. To Briscoe, the majority of boys were from the working class and that was where they were destined to stay. In his recollection, Smith was not over-optimistic or idealistic, and neither were the boys. But whatever his personal understanding, Smith reflected the mainstream view that the destiny of 'half-castes' was amongst the skilled labouring classes.[21]

To the institution perceived by Moriarty and Briscoe, Perkins had added his own reactive personality and experiences. The racial rejections stung. The hurts did not glance off as they did some of the other St Francis lads. He brooded. He did not make friends easily outside the home. He had no money for icecream and Cokes. He was not allowed to join the boys' brigade because no one would provide the money for the uniforms. Once the boys were asked to a birthday party and then told to stay outside; he did not receive an invitation to dinner in the home of a white person until he was 21 years of age. The private griefs were rocks thrown into a pond. The ripples were absorbed and vanished, but at the bottom there gathered an ever growing pile of sharp stones.

All my youth, my best years, were taken from me and I regret it bitterly. The hunger and the poverty of it all. Always hungry. Sometimes when I have a meal now I eat too much. Psychological—I eat too much . . . It's that stolen youth. Stolen youth. And that's the saddest thing of all which I'm so bitterly resentful about. I know lots of people say, 'I worked hard all me life and I never even knew youth, I just worked in a factory' or somebody says 'Life was difficult for me too, always lived in Marrickville, it was Struggletown'. Well I'm not talking about that, I'm talking about my life, and my life as I see it was taken from me. And it shouldn't have been.[22]

As well as change there was loss. Perkins had drifted from most of his extended family. Though he remained emotionally close to his mother, physically she was absent. Perkins hungered for Hetti, he yearned for her. He used to visit Vince Copley's mother's house to soak up the atmosphere of the warm kitchen, the familiar things—and grieved for the loss of his own. He lost that most intimate bonding in Arrernte culture which never would, never could return. He was tough and self-reliant, popular with the lads, but at the deepest level he did not communicate with them nor they with him. He neither understood the reason for the endless discrimination, nor held a positive image of Aboriginality. The years in Sydney would bring that. At the age of sixteen he nursed a longing unshared with his closest friends. Life was nothing but struggle. 'I learned nothing and wasted my life.'[23]

Much remained beyond his understanding. Why was Cyril Hampton not allowed to join the navy simply because he was Aboriginal? Why were the 'Balts' of Port Adelaide, the victims of much initial prejudice, accepted after they learned to 'speak English'? Why were the St Francis lads, after Smith departed, only half wanted, dragged out from time to time as the worthy cause but ultimately despised? Why was he being ejected from the home? Though in maturity he recognised that the slights were directed primarily at his Aboriginality, in 1952 his world was deeply affected by then dominant perceptions of Aborigines as congenitally inferior. Though he did not accept that inferiority, discrimination against himself and others was a fact of life.[24]

Among the change and the loss there was also gain. In raising the boys amongst whites, Smith had imparted the ability to function in their society which life on the

Aboriginal stations could not give. His teachings reinforced the values of honest endeavour. Charles Perkins was only the best known of the St Francis House achievers. Cooper became an industrial foreman, Espie a police sergeant, Briscoe a historian, Copley a chairman of Tandanya Cultural Centre in Adelaide and Moriarty a director of Aboriginal Affairs in South Australia. Perkins, Briscoe and Moriarty are university graduates. The boys' achievements, especially when compared to those in similar institutions, are remarkable.

But Perkins, who in 1952 was grateful for his 'rescue' from the slums of Alice Springs, was much less so by 1988. To him the story of St Francis House is one of opportunities lost, not won. The apprenticeship which was arranged for him he sees merely as a futile limitation on what he might have achieved if the expectation had been that the boys could succeed at anything they tried. Instead, he was expected to fail. While Smith did not say explicitly that Perkins was stupid, he absorbed that estimation in both school and home. He is conscious of his inadequate grasp of English compared to what might have been: 'Combine language with knowledge and you're unbeatable.' Instead, life at St Francis was boring and pointless. After Saturday lunch there was nothing to do but walk for miles along the beaches, grey water under a yellow sky, throwing stones at roofs or rival gangs, walking on brick walls, stealing fruit from trees, aimlessly mucking about. 'I forgive but I don't forget . . . I owe nothing to the whites in Australia. Nothing.'

Some of the St Francis boys feel that there has been a rift between Perkins and themselves in recent years. It may be so. Some were upset when he mentioned the beatings and discomforts of the home in his 1975 autobiography A *Bastard Like Me*. Everyone admitted that they happened, but there was a feeling that they should not have been made public. Perkins conceded that Smith had acted out of kind motives but argued that such things should never be repeated. He began to disentangle himself from the aura of Percy Smith earlier than some of the other St Francis House boys and to that degree he estranged himself from them. In 1975 Perkins was beginning to glimpse more clearly the different contexts in which St Francis House might be placed. In 1988 he was angry that Smith could not see a society racked by the very presence of the invaders:

> There was conflict, turmoil and trauma, and in amongst all of that Father Smith just rode in, and for all the goodness that he had, he drew the wrong conclusions. What he did was for the best of reasons, but his assessment was incorrect.

To Perkins, parents like Hetti who agreed to their children's removal were hoodwinked by the society which allowed the atrocity of separation to occur. Perkins was angry at the regimentation, the lack of counselling about schoolwork, about homework, about life. He reasoned that Smith protected, fed and physically did what he could for the boys, but he could not replace a mother's love. Ultimately, of course, the implications are not Smith's but Australia's. 'How many Aboriginal parents have cried their way to their graves?' he asked in 1988. 'The crimes of ignorance will haunt the nation until Australia pays its dues.' In 1988 Perkins was beginning to understand the dual meaning of institutionalisation.

The removal of his heritage and culture was the other loss whose significance Perkins did not grasp until many years after he left the Home. Did the years away rob him and the other boys of their culture? Is the part-Aboriginal heritage lost in childhood fully recoverable? Is it worth recovering? Should all separated children, whether their parents assented or not, be counted amongst the 'Stolen Generations'? The questions are those which unnumbered Aboriginal children raised by whites still ask themselves. Few find answers.

The questions are particularly acute to the boys of St Francis. Many of them revere Smith as the saint who rescued them from the race hatreds and slums of Alice Springs and raised them to be independent and self-supporting adults. Smith saw few ethical problems either in breeding 'the colour out of the Australian native' or giving his boys a new start 'as normal Australian boys and girls'. Very few did in his generation. The doubts were raised in the children he taught, who, as adults, began to retrace the steps they would have taken had they been allowed to remain within their own culture. Was Smith, the loved father figure, and one of the most caring missionaries ever to take charge of Aboriginal children, also an agent of a much older policy which, whatever its intentions, acted to extinguish the culture of the indigenous people? The steps of recognising and ultimately accommodating the contradictions require an enormous effort of imagination and intellect. The pilgrimage towards an Aboriginal identity, which requires the unlearning of twenty or thirty years of well-meant propaganda, in a mainstream society which continues subconsciously to hate and fear Aboriginality, is as difficult a journey as one may take in modern Australia.[25]

Vince Copley felt that Smith was an assimilationist who was not pleased when the boys in later years supported Aboriginal causes. Espie remembers Smith often telling them, 'I'm glad you boys never went back to the Alice to live, otherwise you'd have undone everything we did for you.' He believed Smith was pleased that he had married a white woman. John Moriarty is more conscious of Smith's love for the boys. If it were a fault that he treated them as 'coloureds' he gave everything he had to their welfare. If the children suffered for their Aboriginality (as they did), he believed it was the fault of society, not Smith's. As in other matters, Perkins is the most bitter at what he lost. He believes that

Aboriginal culture was not a priority for Smith. After the Christmas holidays it was 'just business as usual' at St Francis:

> If I'd stayed [at Alice Springs] I would've been involved more deeply, in a traditional sense. We [St Francis boys] were taken away too, only ours is a sort of a voluntary takeaway, in ignorance. We were taken away too, and the end result is the same. We lost our mothers, and come back for six weeks at the end of the year. At the end of that time, you're gone. Once you've taken an apprenticeship you stay there. Once you're taken away, taken to an institution like that, the effect is exactly the same. You go back now and then but it's so temporary. It's more of a passing fancy than anything permanent . . . But one of the things that I never lost was that I had a mother to go back to. I never had a father, but at least I had a mother, and that was my key point of reference. I knew where I stood, and my point of reference could tell me where I stood, what's happened before and what's happening around me. So I was comfortable in all of that. I had no doubts in my life. But in another sense, we're gone. Taken away. My youth was taken from me by Australia, White Australia. When Aboriginal children are separated it dies, it dies: gone for ever, never return, the connection is never made again. You always stay a little bit different. You may want to look down on people, or you may want to act differently, or you may have different values, for good or for bad. But you are different. That's the way it is and that's the way it will always remain.[26]

The road for such children, as Perkins knows well, goes on forever. His thoughts in 1952, at the time of his autobiography *A Bastard Like Me* in 1975, and at the time of the 1988 recordings, were but weigh-stations on the excruciating journey which for the Stolen Generations has no arrival. Perkins believes, as did Smith, that he would not have achieved so much had he remained at Alice Springs. He is undoubtedly correct—in European terms. The boys were thankful for having avoided apparent alternatives to life at St Francis House, that is, becoming Todd River drunks, illiterate stockmen, the street cleaners. 'Use your imagination' said one former inmate in 1979, 'we'd be more likely to be driving cattle or living in a creek-bed'. In 1952 these alternatives falsely implied that human values for part-Aboriginals did not exist outside European society. By the 1980s, when many part-Aboriginals who had remained were occupying positions of considerable power and influence, these alternatives had become false in fact. Perkins, remaining, would clearly have been the most powerful Indigenous personality in a country of strong people. He would have been the chairman of the Central Land Council, Impaaja Television, the Central Australian Aboriginal Congress or Tangentyere Town Council. He could have been a traditional healer, a fully initiated elder, or a kadaitcha of great mystical power. But though angry at what he lost, Perkins's keenest regrets, and his most bitter criticism, are reserved for those who did not allow him to fulfil his potential in the European arenas of education, soccer and politics. Smith's last legacy to Perkins, and perhaps to all the boys of St Francis, was to place the finest achievements of Indigenous society below those of the Europeans. At the heart of the story of St Francis House there lies an enigma which will not be resolved within the lifetime of the boys.[27]

I forgive but I don't forget

In 1989 the second draft of the manuscript of *Charles Perkins: A Biography* was complete and Charles and I began to discuss, page by page, what I had written. An unexpected discussion turned not on my interpretation of his political career, but on his two slightly differing interpretations of his time in St Francis House.

All the former inmates I have interviewed are to a greater or lesser degree ambivalent about their institutionalisation. They were told many times that the church had done them a favour by removing them from their Alice Springs environment because they were part-Aborigines, because their destiny lay with the whites, and because the so-called 'full blood' people allegedly did not want them. As they reached manhood, the lads were discouraged from returning home, taking part in demonstrations and from marrying Aboriginal women. As it happened, the St Francis House boys became significant achievers, in European terms, particularly compared to former inmates of institutions like Moore River in Western Australia or the Kinchela Boys Home in New South Wales. To a greater or lesser extent the boys, now 55 or 60 year old men, are grateful for having been removed. Unless they had been taken away from the racist and brutal atmosphere of Alice Springs, they argue, they would have been drunks, or street cleaners, or vagrants in the Todd River.

Yet here was an ambiguity, complicated by the fact that the institution's founder, Father Percy Smith, who loved the boys and successfully preserved an intimate family atmosphere, was recalled to Alice Springs by his bishop. He was replaced by a succession of the kinds of people who often find their way into boys' institutions—martinets and exponents of corporal punishments. Most of Perkins' contemporaries have wondered what they would be like had they remained in their home environments. One former inmate confessed that he could not hear the didgeridoo without reflecting on his lost Aboriginal heritage. Another recalled the tears of his relatives linking the railway line at intervals for hundreds of metres as the train left Alice Springs for Adelaide. A third, emotionally closer to Father Smith, reasoned that any shortcomings in the way the boys were treated in later life reflected the nature of Australian society, not their removal from their environment and family.

Charles Perkins himself has gone further than most of the other former inmates in distancing himself from the Home. He wrote in 1975 his autobiography:

> I felt that I was not good enough, an outsider, that I was not part of that school, I was not part of those people, and I belonged to nothing. White society told me I was white but rejected me. They took our Aboriginal heritage away and made us all drifters in society. They took everything from us and condemned us for existing. It was hard times in the minds of such young people. The government helped us to try and understand and the church confused us even more. I needed, and we all needed a father, but we didn't have one.[28]

His reflections a decade later were much sharper. In a recorded interview he described how an Anglican priest had broken a broom over him for leaving the Home for school via the fire escape. He then reflected

> Oh they've got a lot to answer for, these bastards. And the worst part, they were priests. Anglican priests! I'll for ever have a hatred for Anglicans. I'll never let it go.

But the role of Father Percy Smith, the Anglican minister who asked Hetti Perkins to allow him to take her son to Adelaide, Charles summarised as follows:

> There was conflict, turmoil and trauma, and in amongst all of that Father Smith just rode in, and for all the goodness that he had, he drew the wrong conclusions. What he did was for the best of reasons, but his assessment was incorrect.

And the general policy of child removal Perkins characterised thus:

> How many Aboriginal parents have cried their way to their graves? . . . The crimes of ignorance will haunt the nation until Australia pays its dues.

Perkins wanted a few, apparently minor, changes to this section of the text. In the following sentence he wanted the reference to Smith removed: 'To Perkins, parents like Hetti who agreed to their children's removal were hoodwinked, if not by Smith, by the society which allowed the atrocity of separation to occur.' My sentence 'Smith shared many of the prejudices of his time' he wanted to read 'Smith was a product of his time'. At the point in the narrative when Father Smith returned to Alice Springs, he wanted me to add 'From that point the atmosphere of love and understanding departed with him'. The remarks about what was irrecoverably lost by a child's removal he wanted to let stand. Though a little uneasy, he was prepared to let *his* remark stand that 'Father Smith just rode in, and for all the goodness that he had, he drew the wrong conclusions'. But he was unhappy about *my* mid-point assessment that in later life Perkins had begun emotionally to withdraw from Smith. I had written: 'Earlier than most of the St Francis House lads, he had begun to disentangle himself from the aura of Percy Smith and to that degree had estranged himself from some of the others.' His comment on that was 'Unkind?'. Charles preferred less criticism of Smith and more of the regimentation which the boys suffered after Smith left.

The amendments in a sense were tiny. There was no point in arguing about any of them, particularly since at this point of the book I was trying to describe Perkins' feelings as accurately as possible, not place my own interpretation upon them.

Why did he want the changes? The obvious explanations were that the remarks which he had made on tape a year before no longer reflected his state of mind, and that he was worried about the consequences of his criticism becoming public. Neither explanation is adequate. I believe that Perkins' feelings about the Home and Smith had not changed in that year since the interview. Instead, both sets of thoughts, one critical of Smith, one less so, co-existed in his mind, then and now. The dichotomy was reflected in these half-amendments, the fact that he was allowing himself to criticise Smith, but was uneasy at my doing so. Father Smith, the man who removed him from his mother's care and tried to deprive him of his rightful inheritance as an Aboriginal citizen of Australia, was also the father figure to whom Perkins owed much loyalty, gratitude and love.

Is it possible to analyse the many interpretations of a single event within a single mind? Biographers used to try to capture an essence, to distil an experience into a single comprehensive interpretation. Sometimes they argued that a particular event, often in childhood, was a turning point in personality or later development. Here Charles' subtle amendments were drawing me away from the 'distillation mode' to which I had been, perhaps subconsciously, moving. Interpretation piled upon interpretation, meaning succeeded meaning. The event, and the recollection of the event, were the same, but the feelings, good, bad, intense, distant, warm and cold, all co-existed together.

This was not the only place in the manuscript where Charles had difficulty in defining a precise feeling or attitude. In the course of a year of interviews his phrase 'I don't hate but I don't forgive' became—sometimes—'I forgive but I don't forget'. Both remain at different points in the narrative. Because he had stated that at one time in his life he hated whites very much, I took up the point in a sentence towards the end of the book, 'the deepest part of his psyche could not rid itself of the hatred for what the whites had done to him and his people'. But the original 'hatred', used in an earlier context, remains. Like his conflicting views on the meaning of his institutionalisation, I believe that hatred still dwells within him, co-existing with disgust.

The second or third thoughts concerning his institutionalisation are the most crucial because they touch Perkins most deeply. No doubt in any circumstances he would have pondered the meaning of his own removal; but in the last twenty years institutionalised Aborigines have had to face extraordinarily challenging interpretations of their lives and previous beliefs. Separated children were raised in the conventional wisdom that the whites had done them a favour by removing them. Twenty five years ago there was still only silence, or approval of the policies of child removal. Today, from every direction come books of memoirs, oral history radio programs and television discussions about their iniquities, in which the removers either have not emerged with much credit or their good motives have been held to be irrelevant.[29] In the impassioned attack upon the policies and their agents few have paused to consider the traumas which may be imposed upon adults who still revere some of those agents with love and their first, Aboriginal, environment as something they were lucky to have escaped from. One of the St Francis boys wept as he described to me how Smith would read to the boys at night before tucking them into bed. New and sometimes unwelcome intellectual demands have been thrust upon the removed children by another generation, some of whom were not removed themselves, and most of whom were not even Aboriginal. The nearest analogy I can draw to the emotional cleft stick in which the former inmates find themselves is the process of rethinking forced upon those white Australian women now in their sixties and seventies, who after congratulating themselves on having seen their husbands retire with honour and their children well educated and employed, are now told by a reassessing younger generation that their lives had been misspent in ministering to a male autocrat or that they had misused their abilities in 'merely' maintaining the household.

Very few of us, black or white, have been able to resolve either of these dilemmas. Our mothers reply 'well we thought we were right' or 'that's the way society was then'. A common reaction to criticism of child removal is 'but the missionaries (state officials/welfare officers) acted out of Christian love and charity. Surely the children would have died if left in their first environment.' If that is our reaction, imagine how very much more painful it is for those removed children, who were raised on a diet of thankfulness for having been separated and feel a genuine sense of love and gratitude for the white people who raised them, who are now told that they should reject these same people as racists. Very few of the removed children have arrived at any kind of synthesis, or fixed position. Almost all continue to simultaneously carry in their heads two or more radically different interpretations, of which the two strongest, in Charles' case, are love for Smith and respect for his achievement, and anger that anyone was removed at all.

7

Calling in the accounts[1]

In May 1995 the Labor government directed the Human Rights and Equal Opportunities Commission to investigate the past and present separation of Aboriginal children from their parents and communities, the need for any changes in current laws and practices, and principles relating to compensation. The President of the Commission, Sir Ronald Wilson, presented the report 'Bringing Them Home' to the Coalition government in April 1997.

The Commission made 53 recommendations.[2] Those relating to reparation included an apology and measures for restitution, rehabilitation and monetary compensation. Cultural measures included the establishment of centres for language, culture and history, and for family tracing/reunion services and the protection of records. Measures for present day rehabilitation included counselling services and the principles of self-determination of Indigenous communities regarding the welfare of their children. It also recommended that the commonwealth should legislate to implement the Genocide Convention and establish a national Indigenous child placement principle.

The government adopted some of these measures for

reparation (this term covers all aspects of redress for victims, including such measures as rehabilitation and compensation) but rejected many others, notably those involving an apology and compensation to individuals. Much of the debate centred on whether the Stolen Generations were legally or morally owed reparation, and whether public opinion would support reparation. In this chapter I consider the questions of responsibility, then consider how one might establish principles on which to base reparation, and finally consider the reparation which is appropriate.

Who is to blame?

It may be argued that the various Aborigines protection and welfare authorities acted under a general express or implicit directive to assimilate Aborigines. Such a defence might not absolve the states themselves from responsibility for enacting such a policy. Apologists may hold also that its officers were not aware that its assimilationist policies were causing immense psychological and physical harm to the children whom they were removing. However there was sufficient information available to officials to alert them to this strong probability. The argument which follows is drawn from records relating to New South Wales 1921–48, but a similar case might be made using records drawn from other periods or states.

These, drawn from the official records, show that the NSW Aborigines Welfare Board had every opportunity to understand the catastrophic consequences of its policy of child separation:

(a) *Leaving the reserves to avoid family break-ups*

The Board's Minutes of Meetings indicate that in 1921 the number of adult Aborigines leaving the Board's managed stations had become sufficiently a problem for the Board to state publicly that those who left would lose entitlement to housing, food and clothing.[3] Privately it admitted that the real cause of the exodus of families from the stations was that parents wished to retain their children rather than have them removed to institutions.[4]

(b) Press criticism

In 1924 the *Sydney Morning Herald* published an article critical of the Board's policy of making it difficult for girls in domestic service to return home to marry Aboriginal men. The *Herald* believed that the separation of girls to preserve their moral welfare was a policy which 'could not commend itself to those who desired to see the Aboriginal race preserved'.[5] Though the Board replied that 'the extinction of the race was inevitable',[6] it conceded in its next Annual Report that Aboriginal girls 'ought to have a chance to meet people of their own colour'.[7] Yet no administrative machinery was set up to enable the girls to do this.

(c) Complaints by staff

In 1927 Mrs Curry, a former employee of the Cootamundra Girls Home, alleged that girls had been flogged by staff, slashed with a cane across the shoulders and generally treated with undue severity and lack of sympathy. The use of the cane, she alleged, was a daily occurrence.[8] The report was not acted upon due to a 'lack of corroborative evidence'.

In the same year a child welfare inspector reported that the Cootamundra Girls Home Superintendent appeared to be a strict disciplinarian who should show 'a more sympathetic understanding of the girls' maturity and difficulty'.[9] The

Board's records do not indicate that any action was taken on this report.

(d) Ignoring its own statistics

Some 800 New South Wales Aboriginal children were removed from their parents and communities between 1916 and 1928. The majority were girls. My calculations *based on the Board's own records*, indicate that 70 Wiradjuri girls were removed in this period. Of these, nearly *one half* became pregnant to white youths, spent periods in mental hospitals, or died.[10] It is clear that the Board had ample evidence before it to ascertain whether or not its policies were effective both in administrative or humanitarian terms; but the records do not show any attempt made to analyse the statistics in this way.

(e) Abuses at the boys home

A departmental report on the behaviour of the manager of the Kinchela Aboriginal Boys Home, admonished him for taking liquor while in charge of the Home, tying boys to trees and fences, inflicting punishments by stockwhips, hosepipes and deprivation of rations, all without keeping a punishment register.[11] Though a Board member exclaimed that 'the statements of 'these black boys' was 'not worth the paper they were written on', the Kinchela manager was transferred soon after to Cumeroogunga Aboriginal Station.

A former manager of the Kinchela Aboriginal Boys Home stated to a Board internal enquiry that the work the boys were compelled to do, such as scrubbing and washing, was not the life of normal healthy boys.[12] The Board's records do not indicate that any concerted action was taken on this or other very critical reports. Though more boys undertook the Intermediate Certificate, the Kinchela Home remained without such basic amenities as a swimming pool or basketball court until its closure.

(f) Public statements, private policy

The Board's view of child separations was presented in its official magazine *Dawn* in 1953. It claimed to recognise the generally accepted principle that a child's natural heritage was to be brought up in its own home, under the care of its natural parents. It argued that, unfortunately, some parents proved themselves incapable or unsuitable to be entrusted with this duty.[13] At the same time, however, it was common practice to reject parents' request to have their children returned to them even though the initial circumstances (such as the lack of a house or an income) had been remedied. The later whereabouts of State Wards was often kept secret. In 1960 a Cootamundra girl who had done particularly well was to graduate shortly as the state's first Aboriginal nurse. The editor of *Dawn* wanted to place the girl's photograph on the front cover of the magazine. The Board vetoed the plan on the grounds that her family would learn her whereabouts and entice her away.

A case to answer?

In the last 50 years the international community has made considerable progress in legislating for human rights. Several declarations are relevant to the Stolen Generations.

The Universal Declaration of Human Rights

Australia appears to have been in clear violation of the 1949 Universal Declaration of the General Assembly of the United Nations at several points. These include the following:

4. No one shall be held in servitude.

9. No one shall be subjected to arbitrary arrest, detention or exile.

12. No one shall be subjected to arbitrary interference with his privacy, family, home or correspondence . . .

16(3). The family is the natural and fundamental group unit of society and is entitled to protection by society and state.

26(3). Parents have a prior right to choose the kind of education that shall be given to their children.

The Maastricht Seminar, 1992

Relevant findings of the Maastricht Human Rights Project Group include:

6. Every state has the responsibility to redress human rights violations and to enable the victims to exercise their right of reparation.

11. Violations of human rights which entail a right of reparation include genocide, slavery-like practices, disappearances, arbitrary and prolonged detention and systematic discrimination.

12. Victims often suffer from long-term consequences of the wrongs inflicted on them.

16. Compensation is a form of reparation which is to be paid in cash or in kind. The latter may include health and mental health, housing, education and land.

27. Claims relating to violations of human rights should not be subject of a statute of limitations . . . Nobody may be coerced to waive claims for reparation.

17. Non-monetary compensation includes
- verification of facts by public disclosure
- public acknowledgment of responsibility
- bringing to justice of persons found to be responsible
- the holding of commemorations and paying tribute to the victims

- the establishment and sponsoring of institutions for victim after-care.[14]

UN Sub-Commission on Prevention of Discrimination and Protection of Minorities, 1992

The Special Rapporteur, Final Report on the Right to Restitution, concluded:

> 17. Indigenous Peoples. Existing and emerging international law lays special emphasis on the collective rights of indigenous peoples to protection against relocation, and to just and fair compensation for lands which have been confiscated, or occupied. Compensation shall preferably take the form of lands of quality, quantity and legal status equal to those lands which were lost.[15]

Royal Commission into Aboriginal Deaths in Custody

As well as international considerations and rulings, there is also much legal and bureaucratic Australian evidence on the long-term effects of removing Aboriginal children.

The Commission found that 43 of the 100 individuals whose deaths were investigated had been subjected to some kind of juvenile separation, often directly responsible for setting in train the events which led to death in adult life. The Commissioner for New South Wales found that:

> The horror of a regime that took young Aboriginal children, sought to cut them off suddenly from all contact with their families and communities, instil in them a repugnance of all things Aboriginal, and prepare them harshly for a life as the lowest level of worker in a prejudiced white community, is still a living legacy amongst many Aboriginals today.[16]

Statistical correlation

Ninety per cent of the clients seeking assistance from the Victorian Legal Service for criminal charges in 1976 had been in substitute placement at some time in their lives.[17]

Public opinion

While it is true that public opinion is often assumed to be against reparation, it is also true that public opinion in this area has until recently been very poorly informed. When people are given information about the practice and its effects, judgments can change quickly.

An exhibition (*Between Two Worlds*) illustrating the history of separated children in the Northern Territory was mounted by the Australian Archives in 1993. A book inviting visitors' comments was available at each of the six major or capital cities during the exhibition's tour in 1994–95. 15,000 written comments were received from some 100,000 visitors. The following are examples drawn from the Alice Springs venue typical in tone and emotion:

> Moving display that makes me so angry. Every step to inform people is worthwhile.
> Very much an eye-opener to the cruelty of my forefathers. How do you begin to repair or make amends for the stupidity demonstrated?
> [One] May look at Aboriginal people and stand in bitter judgment without ever considering the cruelty, disempowerment and inhumanity shown by 'white' Australians. Unfortunately these prejudices are not dead—I still hear these value judgments.[18]

Principles of reparation

Having established that there is a case to answer, and, at least potentially, a public willing to support reparation, how can we establish the basis on which such reparation could be made? The following are suggested principles on which to base a program of reparation:

Equality after equal deprivation

Whatever their subsequent experience, all separated people suffered equally by the initial deprivation of land, language, culture and family.

Limitation upon restoration of culture

Certain separated adults can never have restored to them what they lost, for example, land, loss of feelings of self-confidence or self-worth, or older family members. They present a special area of consideration.

Threefold area of reparation

Reparation should be made to individuals, who lost family, home and culture; to communities, which lost leadership and cultural continuity; and to the Aboriginal nation which lost numerous opportunities for advancement through the separation of up to one third of its members.

Reparation to be distinguished from other Indigenous programs

It is repugnant, unjust and unprincipled for reparation payments to be met through offsets to allocations for Indigenous programs. Compensation should be met by payments specifically distinguished from these appropriations.

Reparation to restore land to separated people

Separated individuals are at present de facto denied entitlements to land under Native Title legislation. Reparation should therefore encompass compensation for deprivation, *and* redress inequity caused through enforced absence.

Reparations to be seen as equity

Special provisions for separated people should be seen not as arising out of pity or remorse, but out of the demands of justice, equity and a fair entitlement for re-empowered Aborigines.

Variety of mental and material consequence of separation

Separated children, in addition to losing culture and land, are later subject to many other problems, including declining physical or mental health, financial and employment insecurity, uncertainty of identity, and behavioural disorders.

Areas of reparation

In considering what reparation is necessary and appropriate, we need to consider the effects of child removal on individuals, Aboriginal communities, and the Aboriginal Nation as a whole. All have been severely affected in different ways.

Owing to individuals

Individuals suffered at first equally, by being deprived of their culture and family life; later they suffered unequally in subsequent experience. Today, whatever their experiences, all lack access to a family network, land, genealogical and historical information and family life. Measures to restore equal opportunity, such as fast-tracking requests for passports, pensions etc, should be regarded as restorative rather than as reparations.

- All of life pension—Overseas governments, such as the German and Dutch, pay pensions to certain nationals and others in consideration of harsh experiences in the Second World War. Australia pays extra benefits to ex-servicemen and women to whom it owes a special debt. By extension, Australia should pay a special benefit to those whom it especially harmed.

  This has the advantage of being a calculable figure on available numbers, and it follows the principle of 'Equality through equal deprivation'. On the other hand an unknown number have not yet identified as having been separated. To be determined would be issues such as children whose mothers asked the state to care for them, children who were separated but raised by close kin, descendants of removed people yet unborn, and descendants of separated adults who were removed as whole families and relocated to, for example, Palm Island.

- Lump sum compensation in cash—Financial compensation is the normal form of compensation for non-Aboriginal Australians for injuries inflicted by the state or other individuals. A lump sum payment would demonstrate most clearly the government's good faith, and is the most likely to satisfy the demands of separated adults. However a monetary figure is normally arrived at after detailed consideration of the individual case by a court or tribunal and the cost of tribunals would be greater than cash payments. A decision would also be needed on whether the sum was payable to parents and to descendants of removed people.

- Compensation in land—Land is the first spiritual require-
  ment of Aboriginality. Compensation by land grants
  would solve some of the problems outlined above because
  funds could be made available through a body similar to
  the Land Fund Commission. Land would be transferable
  to descendants, and it could be purchased either in areas
  of traditional family identification or elsewhere. Resentment by non-removed Aborigines is possible unless
  similar compensation is made simultaneously in accord-
  ance with principles of ATSIC's 'Recognition, Rights and
  Reform'. It would need to be decided whether such land
  should be alienable.
- Retention of the right to sue—A citizen's right to sue and
  be sued is a fundamental principle of common law which
  enables particularly affected individuals the right to an
  individual hearing (Maastricht Seminar conclusion 27).
  However, the government may demand an estimate of
  costs in advance of legislation, which very difficult in
  advance of judicial findings.

Owing to communities

Communities have suffered through the break up of extended
families, lack of leadership, difficulties of rehabilitating
traumatised returning individuals, and deprivation of local
and family history.

- Training courses for cultural re-education officers—Two-
  or three-week training courses are recommended for individuals who are already working in mental health, housing
  co-ops, land councils, women's groups, combining information and counselling skills. Choosing non-separated
  people among trainees would help to re-educate the non-
  separated Aboriginal community. Such courses would
  recognise that community deprivation leaves the initiative

with communities to best re-educate their returning individuals. It is true that many parts of Australian cities no longer have extended families for individuals to return to. Returning individuals may need additional encouragement to approach organisations such as land councils.

• Establishment of regional records/counselling offices— Regional and local history through records and oral history are best provided by families of the areas. Returning individuals should be able to seek local professional advice in their own country. Individuals would feel more confident to seek help within known areas and non-separated individuals could also seek advice and counselling on the best ways to help traumatised individuals. Counsellors could call on local family members to help individuals returning to those families. This approach affirms the principle of natural Aboriginal regions rather than having boundaries dictated by the non-Aboriginal state, shire and local council, but there would be some duplication of services with existing Link-Up agencies. Separated individuals now are scattered throughout areas of basically non-Aboriginal population, and this makes a community approach more difficult.

Owing to the Aboriginal Nation

Compensation by the states and territories All state governments were responsible for removals except the Northern Territory and the Australian Capital Territory. In the Northern Territory, the commonwealth should be held responsible for separations prior to 1976, and the Northern Territory government after that date.

• Establishment of state records offices—Records of separated people drawn from State Ward and adoption agencies, departments of corrective services and hospitals, currently widely scattered, should be pooled and held in a single office in a central location, perhaps within each state Aboriginal Affairs complex. This would make information more easily accessible to separated people living in urban areas.

But there are many difficulties in achieving this aim. They include obtaining records from departments of corrective services and from now defunct adoption agencies, in identifying Aboriginal files in general welfare records, the high cost of Freedom of Information applications, and the need to protect privacy, including for deceased people.

- Establishment and extended support of Link-Up organisations—Link-Up organisations possess the skills, personnel and mechanisms to ensure that record releases, counselling and reunions are carried out sensitively. The Commonwealth government currently provides the bulk of state Link-Up funding, whereas the states have a clear responsibility to contribute a much greater proportion. States should contribute at least 50 per cent of the funding of these organisations, but some do not yet possess independent Link-Up agencies

- Streamlining of Link-Up intra- and inter-state services— Some state Link-Up workers currently must have their requests for records approved by a state welfare employee. Link-Up and Aboriginal Child Care agency workers should be given the same access to files as if they were state employees. Link-Up workers should be appointed whose first priority is clients whose case-histories involve more than one state or territory. Separated people would be accorded equality of opportunity which they still currently lack.

Compensation by the Commonwealth The Commonwealth has a framing, co-ordinating, and enforcing role in affirmative action, equal opportunity and anti-discrimination legislation. The Commonwealth had a highly significant role in separating children in the Northern Territory to 1976.

- An annual national public commemoration or 'sorry day'—The desire for recognition is more important for some separated people than financial compensation. A public day of mourning to commemorate all people involved (extended family, parents, children and descendants), has analogies with Anzac Day, the 1938 Day of Mourning, and NAIDOC week. A national day, especially with a minute's silence, would focus the nation's attention on separated people without distraction of other important issues. It would help educate both the non-Aboriginal community and the Aboriginal non-separated community in the problems of returning separated adults.

- A national commemorative centre or 'sorry place'—A quiet area could be established, possibly in the National Museum, for prayers, flowers and meditation. This would allow a place for contemplation by all those affected by the policies and would help educate all Australians on the very serious consequence of the policies. It would also point to the fact that many separated people and their families can never be found or recognised individually.

- A list of persons affected, or 'roll of honour', in Canberra—There are analogies to the Roll of Honour in the Australian War Memorial, or the Vietnam Memorial in Washington, which also help the recognition of suffering in terms of absolute numbers. But it would be extremely difficult to make a definitive list, some individuals may not want their name included, and a decision made on whether parents and/or descendants would be included.

Joint commonwealth and state initiatives Commonwealth and

states hold joint responsibility for separation policies, and some aspects of reparation demand a joint approach.

- Establishment of a Trust Fund—A Trust Fund similar to the Land Trust Fund could disburse funds in cases of hardship caused by separation, for land purchase, prison rehabilitation, art, literary projects, language study etc. Such a fund would allow all cases to be treated on merit by a tribunal, including consideration of descendants and disburse funds in acknowledgment of special hardship.

8

Sorry Business[1]

The government made its formal response to 'Bringing Them Home' on 16 December 1997. John Herron, Minister for Aboriginal and Torres Strait Islander Affairs, presented a package of $63 million in 'practical assistance', including provision for the Australian Archives to copy and preserve files, the tape recording of life histories, development of family support programs, a national network of Link-Up services, the employment of new counsellors and the expansion of regional counselling centres.[2] The government refused to apologise on behalf of the Australian people (a refusal consistent with earlier comments about 'black armband history' by the Prime Minister), and refused to consider other key aspects of the recommendations of the report, notably compensation.

Criticism of the report was made, obliquely, by the government, and more directly by newspaper correspondents, some columnists and Dr Ron Brunton of the Institute of Public Affairs. Such criticism has helped to form public opinion on the Stolen Generations and on the actions the government should take in response to the whole sorry business. In this chapter I consider the major points made by the critics of the report.

Why didn't the Aboriginal people complain to the newspapers about child removal if it was as bad as they say it was now?

In recent decades there has been little explicit and open information from governments about the child removal programs in various states. Its extent was well hidden. While individuals and families knew what was happening to them personally it was difficult to gain an overall perspective necessary to get the press or government to listen. A story of wrongful removal simply would not have made the national press until the 1980s.

Nevertheless there was much agitation in the 1920s, possibly because governments at this time were much more explicit about their intentions towards the Aboriginal people even in their public documents. Certainly, public Aboriginal opposition to the child removal policy was loudest at that time. The Aborigines Protection Association, an all-Aboriginal lobby group formed in 1925, claimed that 'girls of tender age are torn away from their parents . . . and put to service in an environment as near to slavery as it is possible to find'.[3] Its president Fred Maynard wrote to the New South Wales Premier in 1927, demanding that 'family life of Aboriginal people shall be held sacred and free from invasion and interference and that the children shall be left in the control of their parents'.[4] He did not, however, present separations in the 1990s terms of ethnocide or cultural genocide. Reinforced by white women activists arguing for the general sanctity of the family unit, Maynard's demands were more directed at the preservation of the child–parent bond than preventing the extinction of Aboriginality.[5]

Five years later the child separation plank was off the Aboriginal activists' platform. The reasons are not clear. The successor to the Association, the Aboriginal Advancement League, stood for 'Education, Opportunity and Full Citizen Rights', and though leaders sometimes included separation in correspondence with the premiers, its 1938 ten point program said nothing about the separation of children.[6] One reason, to judge by the headlines in the journal *Abo Call*, was the even more urgent concern that southern Aborigines were being exterminated by loss of land, starvation and ill treatment on the reserves. Another is that many of the children who returned—probably less than 50 per cent—were too traumatised by their experiences, too unsure of their Aboriginal identity, to take a political role.[7]

A third reason may be that while Maynard's Progressive Association, travelling constantly through the country, had remained in immediate touch with grassroots concerns, the 1930s leaders worked amongst the rural communities less frequently and presented their demands in a more universally recognisable form.[8]

In the 1950s the state and territory administrations, while not noticeably reducing the numbers of forced separations, justified their actions with totally new rationales. The intention of governments was no longer to 'eventually solve the Aboriginal problem'. Now the states claimed to recognise the incapacity or unsuitability of certain parents to be entrusted with the duty of looking after their children: the state would have to do it for them.[9] Simultaneously the protest organisations which before the Second World War had been either all-Aboriginal or all-white were replaced with new alignments guided by the principle that since colour prejudice intimately involved both blacks and whites, it would have to be opposed by blacks and whites together. The ironically predictable result was that the more articulate and better educated whites, occupying most of the executive positions of the 'joint' organisations, did most of the public speaking until the end of the 1960s. Possibly some of the more conservative members of the joint 'progress' associations actually approved of separations.

Now for another mystery. While all the post-war advancement organisations were devoted to education, welfare or political progress, none to my knowledge adopted the plank of ending the child separation policy. Few manifestos even mentioned it. Perhaps the whites' own lack of comprehension of the extent of the policy and the cruelty of its execution helped to prevent separation from entering the agenda of serious political intention.

Why didn't decent people protest?

To blame them is easy, to take ourselves back to the understandings of the 1960s needs a greater effort of will. It was almost beyond their—that is, our—comprehension that certain of our own officials of state and church, foster parents and institutional superintendents were acting with the wickedness revealed in 'Bringing Them Home'; nor did we understand the psychological effects of constantly negating Aboriginality before children whom we wrongly assumed would be readily accepted by the rest of society as if they were white.

I suspect that few Indigenous or non-Indigenous people in the 1960s really understood that there was a *policy* of removal at all. Separation had become structural, comparatively invisible. Individual cases which were occasionally publicised seemed to concern individual children who happened to be Aboriginal, in need because their parents, poor things, couldn't cope, and who must be rescued to be given a better chance. Not even all the officials who carried away the children knew that there was a policy. Perhaps they too saw only individuals to be rescued, even though the *sum* effect of mass separations would be to put an end to Aboriginality. The better carers in the institutions believed that all children were the same under the skin.

I too, when I conducted my first interviews with separated people in the mid-1970s, was misled partly through the way in which they constructed their own life histories, and partly through that same misplaced British-derived faith that the state would serve all its citizens honestly and equally. If I had been twenty years older I probably would have joined the Federal Council for the Advancement of Aboriginal and Torres Strait Islanders and supported its policies. I too in 1960 would have considered adopting a 'poor helpless little Aboriginal child'. That was what decent white people did.

Professor Ann Curthoys has argued that white Australian feminists had difficulty in recognising their own complicity in the racist context within which Aboriginal people work and live. Their own self-perception had cast womanhood as that of victim, making it extremely difficult for them to conceptualise themselves as the oppressors of Aborigines which they were. From this position Curthoys proposed that our wider self-perception makes it difficult for all non-Aboriginal Australians to see themselves as oppressors of Aborigines.[10] Our national mythology is that of the battler, the individual almost overwhelmed by the weather or banks or government. We think of the nation itself as a battler against more powerful nations or foreign misfortunes. It is not so easy to see ourselves as an oppressor of fellow Australians.

But ignorance and misplaced faith are not sufficient explanations either. A number of Aboriginal newspapers flourished in the 1960s, which also gave very few indications that Aboriginal children were being separated at all, still less as an act of aggressive government policy. Partly it remained a matter of priorities. White supporters pushed hardest for what they best knew: better education, equal wages, workers' rights, political equality, retaining the reserves, the elimination of malnutrition, poor health and housing. Aboriginal leaders also, mostly male, raged against what they best knew and what they had experienced themselves: massacres, forced marriages, hated managers and lost land, not lost children. It was not until 1972 that the wise Kevin Gilbert pinpointed forced family disintegration as a deliberate act of the white administrations:

> The Acts empowered government departments to remove whole families from reserves and send them to any area—often hundreds of miles from their tribal country. Children were forcibly removed from their parents and sent as slaves to other areas, often never to see their parents again. Husbands were removed from their families, wives from their husbands.[11]

The long silence of the concerned blacks and whites was compounded and assisted by the public silence of the people concerned. The removed children and their parents were absent from the national debates during the decades from the 1930s to the 1960s. The desperate efforts of many families to keep them, and their childrens' later struggles against their coercive employers, were conducted in private (with the help of a few equally obscure but valiant white sympathisers) against administrations which as often as not sent the troublemakers off to jails and mental asylums. Their histories still are mostly confined to collections of family letters and PhD theses. The masculinist political discourse of the 1960s remained, as it had in the later 1930s, not families but economics, wages, civil rights, land, education. To grieving parents separation implied a lack of their own care. Many an adopting mother accepted the hospital matron's admonition not to be selfish because their child had a much better chance with a 'lovely middle-class white family'.

There were Aboriginal people writing in the 1970s. Why didn't they complain about their treatment?

Institutionalisation was still, in the 1970s, generally regarded as a profoundly beneficial experience by those who endured it. In the mid-1970s, a few were prepared to describe the psychological and physical pain of separation, institution or asylum, but their resentment was directed at their own family, not the actions of disturbed white officials nor the policy itself. The Stolen Generations had still to free themselves from an imposed psychological bondage which portrayed their separation as inevitable, beneficial or subsequent to parental neglect. That process, which coincided with the development of the Link-Up movement, continued throughout the 1980s and 1990s.

As we have changed, so have the Stolen Generations themselves. They have aged, and become more reflective about their lives, and they have more information on which to reflect. Accounts they give now present a much harsher and accusing account of their separation than they did in the 1970s.

Can we trust oral history?

If an individual's own perceptions of his or her past change, can they be relied upon? Much recent debate about the nature of oral history has crossed into personality theory, and the extent to which self-perceptions (and therefore self-presentations) alter during the whole of the life cycle. Does that mean that only one narrative of separation is correct? If so, which one? If the separated children tell different stories at different times of their lives about their removal, the critics of 'Bringing Them Home' may ask, why must we accept the ones which present separation in the worst light?

The answer is that the written records uphold them. The files still held by the state administrations almost uniformly support the most harrowing of the verbal accounts which together explode the myth that institutionalised children somehow were better off for having been separated.

As part of a court case, I was asked to examine the case histories of ten Aboriginal people all removed from the same area within a ten year period. Every single one of them declined catastrophically in both personality and intelligence as they were then measured. Not a single child remained, in character, behaviour or intellect at anything like the first optimistic levels of the early institutional reports. The following comments are drawn from school reports and superintendents' assessments.

Herbert
1947: 'a very satisfactory type of boy', of 'good conduct'
1951: 'erratic, somewhat irrational and a little violent'

Clem
1943: first in a class of six
1947: 'a very good worker by himself'
1953: convicted of assault and robbery

Elsie
1946: 'good conduct'
1947–48: encouraging school reports
1949: 'very poor intelligence', special abilities 'nil'

1950: 'a very lazy worker and not clean', 'seems to be in a daze'

George
1941: 'Trustworthy', 'very good'
1944: 'very dull'
1946: 'spends all his spare time on his bed reading and sleeping'

Norman
1944: 'a good little boy', 'satisfactory', 'very bright'
1950: 'difficult', 'temperamental', 'very erratic', 'of doubtful morals and honesty'
1952: of insufficient education even to join the army

Fred
1947: 'satisfactory, developing along the right lines'
1951: 'very sullen disposition', 'most unhappy'

Claude
1946: 'intellectually good', 'fair', 7th in a class of 12
1950: 'unsettled' after running away to join his mother
1952: certified insane and placed in a mental hospital

Betty
1943–45: 'good little worker' 'willing and bright' who 'tries to take the lead and should do well'
1952: 'lazy', 'of filthy habits', 'not amenable to discipline', 'quite beyond human endurance'

Annie
1942: first in class, behaviour 'very fair even good', needs help, 'wants to be a nurse'
1943: 'reasonably good'
1949: 'defiant, rude and untruthful', legally uncontrollable

Irene
1945: did well in some subjects at school
1946: 'good child', 'doing all right', 'good'

1948: 8th out of a class of 21, although of 'poor' intelligence; 'doing very well', 'a good willing girl'
1950: accused of theft, 'tantrums', complained of loneliness
1952: 'mentally retarded', 'should be examined by a mental expert'
1962: 'in and out of gaol, mostly for drunkenness'.

All this information was drawn from the authority's own records.

In all of the current politicised debate, many fail to accept that the alternative for many Aboriginal children was a sentence to a dismal lifestyle with very poor health prospects. [12]

A great deal of the poor health and dismal lifestyle which Aboriginal people experienced was not alleviated but *caused* by the so-called Aborigines Protection Boards themselves. The worst malnutrition, the deepest boredom, the most decrepit housing commonly occurred on the very stations which were controlled and overseen by the state authorities.

Contrast the history of two Aboriginal living areas in south-central New South Wales. The Aborigines of Narrandera lived from 1925 to 1940 in tin huts of their own construction in an area eight kilometres from the town, known as the Sandhills. There were no rations, shops, transport, running water, electricity or school. From this unofficial settlement not a single Aboriginal child was removed in fifteen years. The residents of Cowra Aboriginal station, by contrast, lived in wooden houses built by the Aborigines Protection Board, with a stove, community taps, church, school, rations, all supposedly maintained by the manager. In the same period, at least a dozen children were removed. Similar examples can be multiplied from all over the country. Aboriginal children were separated not only to 'rescue' them from unalleviated malnutrition but because station managers used separation as a tool of control and punishment.

The alternative of having children moved into better circumstances was an attractive one for concerned parents.[13]

Some parents did ask the authorities to care for their children for a time, and a few thoughtful adopting parents and institutional carers made sure that the children kept their contacts with their own families by encouraging visits and letters.

But the parents who handed their children to the authorities often did so understanding that they would be returned to them as soon as home circumstances improved. They were not returned. After reading all the thousands of childcare records of the NSW Aborigines Protection Board, I can think of many instances of parents asking unsuccessfully for their children to be returned, but not of a single instance where the child actually was returned. The authorities exploited some parents' desire for a temporary transfer by breaking their side of the agreement.

The churches and government authorities genuinely thought that this was a beneficial and kindly procedure[14]

Governments and churches certainly did not always act with the best of motives, nor until the 1950s, did they bother about concealing them. Consider these extracts drawn from government or bureaucratic sources:

New South Wales 1921

> . . . the continuation of this policy of dissociating the children from camp life must eventually solve the Aboriginal problem forever.[15]

Western Australia 1904

> [A] half-caste who possesses few of the virtues and nearly all the vices of the whites, grows up to be a mischievous and very immoral subject . . . it may appear to be a cruel thing to tear an Aborigine child from its mother, but it is necessary in some cases to be cruel to be kind.[16]

Northern Territory 1930s

Generally by the fifth and invariably by the sixth generation, all native characteristics of the Australian aborigine are eradicated. The problem of our half-castes will quickly be eliminated by the complete disappearance of the black race, and the swift submergence of their progeny in the white . . .[17]

Queensland 1930s

> [The Queensland Act allowing the removal of children] should include the illegitimate children of half-caste mothers, the children of parents both half-castes . . . reported . . . to be living in low conditions and a menace to health and discipline.[18]

Queensland 1960

> . . . the Government is not going to allow white and near

white children whether their parents are black or white to remain on the Settlements at the cost of the tax payer.[19]

Naturally there were some sympathetic police, kindly administrators and gentle church people. But while the churches were no worse than the state in obtaining children and implanting them with shame and disgust at their Aboriginality, they were entirely complicit in their co-operation with the secular desire of government to break up Aboriginal families. These are the words of the famous Victorian missionary Hagenauer about an Aboriginal family which the Victorian Aborigines Protection Board was trying to evict from a station:

> The Board cannot grant rations to Henry Albert and family as they are half-castes, but every assistance will be given to place their children into the Industrial Schools and get them boarded out to respectable families.[20]

Sometimes, indeed, the church missions were criticised by the state itself for being over-zealous:

> The Mission representatives say that if the girls are left in the bush they only become the prey of white men and become mothers at a very early age. My experience has been removing them to towns and to institutions does not overcome this trouble and only accentuates and increases it.[21]

Just as some church people were admirable, some were despicable. Consider 'Bringing Them Home' confidential evidence No. 557:

> . . . Sister A, poor thing, who's dead—I know she was upset because the priest that had that young girl living in his place. He used to come and get her out of the dormitory every night. He used to sneak in about half past twelve, one o'clock in the morning and take her. We'd get up in the morning and she'd be just coming in the door.[22]

Neither the policy statements nor oral history demonstrate that governments acted 'at most times with the very best of motives'.[23]

You can't judge past practices by today's standards[24]

Critics of the day condemned separation by the standards of their own day, not ours. 'Bringing Them Home' quoted this report from the newspaper *Queenslander* written more than 100 years ago:

> the aboriginal inhabitants are treated exactly in the same way as the wild beasts or birds the settlers may find there . . . Their goods are taken, their children forcibly stolen, their women carried away, entirely at the caprice of the white men.[25]

Nor was criticism confined to journalists. This is an extract from a Report of the Queensland Chief Protector of Aboriginals himself:

> Kidnapping of boys and girls is another serious evil . . . Boys and girls are frequently taken from their parents and their tribes, and removed far off whence they have no chance of returning.[26]

Aboriginal parents have never concealed their feelings from the authorities. This letter, for example, was sent to the Protector of Aboriginals in Alice Springs in April 1941:

> I myself, and my wife, both half castes we understand, do not want any of our children removed, out of this Central Australia their country.
> It would not be fair to us, the loss of them. Also not

fair to them, the loss of their parents, causing crying and
fretting . . .

Will you please *place* this *Protest*, as we do not understand any *forcible* removal, of any of us, from this Central
Australia, our birthright country.[27]

There has never been a time in Australia when the
separation policy was not strongly criticised.

**[The Minister] wanted to know more about
others involved in the process, including
missionaries, administrators, police and
adoptive and foster parents. 'For a complete
understanding we need to know their
motivations and their perceptions, as well.'[28]**

What underpinned almost all the separations perpetrated by
church and state, and of many hundreds of well meaning
adopting parents, was the general principle that Aboriginality
itself was worthless. It is this deep, sometimes unconscious,
groundswell of conviction which Aboriginal people find hardest to forgive. It underlay every policy, every action. This
extract is from J. Devaney's *The Vanished Tribes*, recommended
reading for the New South Wales Sixth Class in the 1941
curriculum. That principle of Aboriginal worthlessness, so
entrenched in this last generation of Australians to carry out
mass separations, is here embodied in every phrase and adjec-
tive:

I say, Dick, he called, 'Who's the greasy old buck nigger
outside here?' . . .

'That's old Koorooma, one of the local nigs . . . He's the
last of his tribe, a crazy, harmless old coot, but one can't do
anything for him, that's the trouble.'

'Cadging tucker, of course' said Sitherley. 'Darn the abos, they were always but a confounded nuisance everywhere, and it's best for us and themselves that they're just about finished.'[29]

Parents and children alike may choose to recall more congenial family circumstances than actually existed.[30]

Some do, though bad memories of life on the reserves as infants also keeps Aboriginal adults from returning home or even confronting their memories. It is true also that some institutions provided relatively gentle and safe environments for separated Aboriginal children. Sally Morgan's mother Gladys, placed in the institution Parkerville in Perth, evidently recalled with gratitude the bush and the birds, the trips to the pictures and the zoo.[31] Whether such institutional life was better or worse than that which replaced it, is irrelevant. Aboriginal children were entitled to an Aboriginal home life.

Sometimes alcohol or sexual abuse rendered home life impossible. Most of Australia's child welfare Acts now require authorities, in such circumstances, to seek alternative *Aboriginal* placements beginning with the close kinfolk. That these compulsory provisions did not exist before 1980 indicates not that the extended kin networks were unwilling to care for other children, but that the authorities did not want them to.

Harrowing anecdotes are used in an attempt to force compliance with the report's recommendations[32]

Not 'to force compliance'. A statutory commission like the

Human Rights and Equal Opportunity Commission cannot 'force compliance' on anybody. But the inference remains that Commissioners relied too heavily on spoken testimony in the absence of corroborative written evidence.

Each chapter of Part II of 'Bringing Them Home' (dealing with state histories) has a comprehensive documentary history of the separation policy, almost all drawn from public documents such as annual reports. As a Link-Up field worker I routinely, with permission, obtained the file of every person whom I was asked to help find family and Aboriginality. I can think of only one instance of hundreds where the record did not closely corroborate the individual's own narration.

Here is one of the hundreds of 'harrowing anecdotes' contained in 'Bringing Them Home', in which a Victorian Koori related how he began stealing:

> I reckon all my trouble started when I was living in them homes. That's when I first started stealing because you wasn't allowed to have anything and if I wanted something the only way I could get it is get it off someone else, get me brother or sister to buy it or just take it. We were sort of denied everything we wanted, just got what was given and just be satisfied with that. I felt second-rate. I didn't feel like I got the love I was supposed to get; like a kid's supposed to get at that age, because they're more vulnerable at that age. They just follow people that seem to look more after them. That's why I got in with the wrong crowd, I suppose. They seemed to care.[33]

The written records of the State Archives directly or indirectly support such 'harrowing anecdotes'. The following extract indicates how depriving an adolescent of love and self-confidence is likely to turn a normal child into an abnormal adult.

The extract is the section marked 'Disposal' which was the

last entry of the one-page record kept by the NSW Aborigines Protection Board on each of its wards.[34] Note the final comment that the ward, at the age of twenty, and after three or four years in a mental institution, has returned to her family, perhaps thereby to confirm what 'everybody knew' about the emotional instability of part-Aborigines. Yet by another interpretation this woman had been driven insane by the state itself.

The girl left the Cootamundra Girls Home for an intended position in domestic service at the age of fifteen: but she only lasted there five days.

Disposal Transferred from Cootamundra to Longueville [Sydney suburb] 9.2.28. Sydney Rescue Home 14.2.28; Brewarrina Aboriginal Station 17.2.28; service at Rowena [pastoral property] 6.5.28; returned to Brewarrina 17.6.28; service at Avondale [pastoral property] 21.7.28, unmanageable, sent to police station Collarenebri; taken charge by sister 21.12.28; taken Reception House [asylum] 24.1.29; transferred Urunga Aboriginal Station 5.2.29; service at east Bellingen, 11.2.29, uncontrollable; returned Urunga 4.2.29; tried again at service 6.4.29, again became uncontrollable and violent, sent back to station; brought to Sydney and admitted Reception House. Admitted Callan Park Mental Hospital by order of Court, 1.5.29; 1933 heard that she had returned to Darlington Point and living with sister.

Were there no happy outcomes, no adoptive families that grew in strength through the nurture of a 'stolen' child, no lives shaped successfully from orphanage beginnings that might have taken a different course in a tribal environment hostile to half-castes?'[35]

Of course there were. Many adopted children remained very

close to their adopting parents. The majority of adopting parents took Aboriginal children from honourable motives and tried very hard to make the adoption work. Some remain perplexed to this day that it did not. But the fact that there were and are loving and unprejudiced adopting parents, and dedicated foster and institutional carers is not the point. Discrimination against Aborigines in the society *outside* the home was never far away, and a close and loving family was no more able than an unloving one to provide an Aboriginal support network in that hostile world.

The proportion of home and institutional placements which broke down is very much greater than those which succeeded. There's no doubt that Aboriginal life in country towns was generally made pretty rough even in the 1970s. But there is also no doubt that Aboriginal children who grew up with their families in these towns are today stronger and better adjusted adults than those who did not.

The authors of ['Bringing Them Home'] must have known that in the '30s there was very strong Aboriginal support for incorporation into white society.'[36]

The Indigenous leaders of the 1930s did not agree on everything, including the ultimate fate of Aborigines living in southern Australia. Nevertheless, it is easy to misread their speeches and writings.

Those who make this assertion base their evidence on the Australian Progressive Association's six-issue broadsheet *Abo Call*. This is one extract frequently cited:

> So far all Aborigines in Australia who want the privileges and benefits of civilisation for the welfare of their wives

and children should get behind this movement. Say goodbye to the damper and ashes, and to the compounds! We want to be absorbed into the Nation of Australia and thus survive in the land of our forefathers, on equal terms.[37]

The key word in this passage by the New South Welshman Bill Ferguson is 'survive', for that was the focus of all the 1930s spokespeople. The editorial from which this quotation is selectively quoted is not a request for assimilation but a savage attack upon the reserve system which kept Aboriginal people prisoners. A fiery sentence shortly before this passage reads 'the wrecking of our physical condition through inadequate food supplies, has only one object—Extermination!'.

The Aboriginal leaders intended to end the abusive and oppressive reserve system by the only means that seemed feasible at the time—the eventual abolition of the reserves and their hated managers.

It could be seen as somewhat ironic that many who are now protesting about the issue are only alive today because of the fact that they were given a chance of survival from the appalling conditions they would otherwise have had to face.[38]

Archival records reveal that authorities sometimes left houses unrepaired in order to *force* people to leave the reserves, or to provide an excuse for removing the children. Nor has any Aboriginal national leader separated as a child, whatever their circumstances, claimed that their removal from their own family was the better option. Surely the irony is in the way in which the separated children have turned the education they were given not to become better non-Aborigines, but to use those skills in the service of their people.

[T]he government does not support an official national apology. Such an apology could imply that present generations are in some way responsible and accountable for the actions of earlier generations, actions that were sanctioned by laws of the time, and that were believed to be in the best interests of the children concerned.[39]

We've already seen that at certain periods in our history, the 'protection' authorities did not conceal the fact that the separation laws were in the interest of the whites, not the Aboriginal children. One of the basic tenets of responsible government is that successive administrations are responsible for the financial and other decisions of their predecessors. Without that understanding government could not proceed.

An apology does not necessarily imply responsibility for the past; rather it acknowledges that actions and policies once thought right (or at least, utilitarian) by government now are revealed to have been wrong. An apology should express this belated realisation to those affected Australians. Only the Australian government can apologise on behalf of all Australians.

Also it is hurtful to the many decent people who adopted or cared for Aboriginal children to carry their burden of responsibility alone, while the federal government continues to slip from its own historical role. Such people were assured by the state that adoption met its approval; sometimes their child's Aboriginality was deliberately concealed from them. Now they need reassurance that their actions were not wicked but mistaken. Since the report, non-Aboriginal Australians have enough to carry in the knowledge of what they have done intentionally or unintentionally without bearing also the weak and immoral evasions of governments which sanctioned and encouraged the separations.

That [Japan's atrocities in World War II] was war and this wasn't.[40]

Yes it was. How can 20,000 Aboriginal dead, over 50,000 children deprived of an Aboriginal identity, and thousands of adults forcibly evicted from camps and reserves to end their association with each other, be anything but war? There is only peace when opposing sides agree that there is peace, and Aborigines have never done so. On the contrary, there was war because the Aboriginal people felt it to be so. Listen to William Ferguson in the 1930s.

> If you would openly admit that the purpose of your Aborigines Legislation has been, and is now, to exterminate the Aborigines so completely so that not a trace of them or of their descendants remains, we could describe you as brutal, but honest. But you dare not admit openly that what you hope and wish for is our death! You hypocritically claim that you are trying to 'protect' us; but your modern policy of 'protection' (so called) is killing us off just as surely as the pioneer policy of giving us poisoned damper and shooting us down like dingoes![41]

9

In the courts: 'In the middle of the ocean, drowning'[1]

In the best interests of the children

Research amongst urban Aborigines in the 1980s emphasised difference where previously little difference between urban whites and blacks was believed to exist.[2] Today, anthropologists realise that urban Aborigines and non-Aborigines, while seeming to follow similar life-styles, in reality differ profoundly in such matters of history, experience, language, kin-structure, world-view, child-rearing practice, attitudes and methods of dispute-settling. That's why Aboriginal children have the right to be raised in an Aboriginal environment, or if they come from a mixed marriage, then they are entitled to live within an Aboriginal culture for part of the time.

Mixed marriages, like others, break down and children are liable to be raised principally by one of the parents. Such children still possess, and are morally entitled to share, the separate set of relatives and the separate history, experience, value-system and world view to which their Aboriginal descent entitles them.

Will raising a child mainly by its Aboriginal parent lead to an analogous alienation from non-Indigenous value-systems? This is much less likely because Aboriginal children are already surrounded by such values in schools, work-places, recreational and sporting venues. Aboriginal children raised in their own culture have a knowledge of, and often respect for, the wider culture. The inequalities and prejudice still existing in Australian society ensure that the placement of a part-Aboriginal child with its Aboriginal parent is much more likely to lead to a balanced and constructive citizen than placement with its white parent.

Placing a child for at least equal time with its Aboriginal parent or grandparent means that it is much less likely to be discriminated against in the family home. If discrimination does occur in the wider society, the child will have a network of psychological support from the Aboriginal home and community unavailable in the white household. And the child is more likely to grow up as a constructive and well-balanced adult if it has a positive self-image as Aboriginal, and has learned to deal with discrimination and prejudice.

Yet judges and magistrates sometimes appear to believe that neither the numbers of Aboriginal children removed, nor the methods of removal, have any relevance to present day cases before the Australian courts. Furthermore, the belief that a part-descent Aboriginal identity does not exist, or if it exists, does not matter, continues to pervade white Australian society. Nevertheless, Aboriginal people continue to assert the right of part-descent people to identify as Aboriginal if certain criteria are fulfilled.

A court order may deprive parents or communities of the right to raise their children as effectively as the seizure of the children generations ago. The survival of Aboriginality is constantly under threat; each child deprived of its birthright to identify as Aboriginal as well as European is another child lost to Australia's Indigenous people.

It is legitimate for the court to recognise that an individual part-Aboriginal child is also a member of a historically persecuted people whose survival as a group depends on each of its members assuming a useful and psychologically balanced identity within the Aboriginal culture. Many removed Aboriginal people, by contrast, have reflected on the traumatic effects of institutionalisation.[3] They became withdrawn, confused and ashamed of their Aboriginal identity, but it was their communities which suffered, in the next generation, from a lack of leadership that would have been enjoyed had the children remained. The Honourable Justice Wootten QC, the New South Wales Royal Commissioner into Aboriginal Deaths in Custody, wrote:

> One cannot spend much time amongst the Aboriginal people of New South Wales without realising the truth of [the alleged harmful effects of separation]. Constantly one meets people whose lives have been shattered or gravely disturbed by the taking away of children. They may have been grandparents or parents or brothers or sisters or other relatives of the people concerned. They may have been the children themselves or they may be themselves the children of those who were taken away, their own lives suffering from the damage that was done to their parents. Many people are still mourning the children that were taken away, or are themselves people who were taken away and are still seeking their relatives. There are many heart rending stories of searches and reunions in the Aboriginal community.[4]

It clearly is legitimate, if not necessary, for Australian courts to redress the balance of child-rearing in favour of Aboriginality because the Aborigines have suffered for so long from the excesses of white authorities in removing their children. A court granting sole custody to a non-Aboriginal parent in a custody dispute may have an exactly similar effect on both the child and its community, as did the seizure of children by more brutal officials a century ago. We may note that the officials of the time thought, as do the modern courts, that they were acting in the best interests of the children.

The most reassuring phenomenon for those who believe in the continued survival of Aboriginality has been the number of removed children, who in past generations may not have known about, still less proclaimed, their Aboriginal descent, but who are now coming forward to take their place as Aboriginal citizens of Australia. Though often traumatised by humiliating or brutal experiences, the returning adults are now a driving force in Aboriginal cultural life.

Yet every member of the Stolen Generations carries psychological damage to some degree. Clearly they were amongst those who experienced Kevin Gilbert's 'rape of the soul' most profoundly. The continuing and never-relinquished claims of Aboriginal adults to raise their own children according to their own culture and belief system entitle them to prior consideration in every court and tribunal in the land.

Some observations on the trial and sentencing of Russell Moore

In November 1989 I was invited by the Victorian Aboriginal Legal Service to join a group of Australians travelling to speak in the defence of Russell Moore, a Victorian Koori who, a year previously, had raped and murdered a woman in Melbourne, Florida. Moore had already been found guilty in a separate trial. Our task was to plead for clemency during the 'penalty phase', under which, in American law, the jury recommends a sentence to the judge.

At the end of the trial the jury recommended a life sentence, which, after our departure, was overruled by the judge imposing the death penalty. Subsequently that decision was overturned by the Florida Supreme Court. Russell Moore was returned to jail to begin his life sentence. Successive Australian governments have showed little interest in having him returned to Australia to serve out his sentence.

Capital punishment is for some Americans an urgent and divisive moral issue in a way it has not been in Australia for more than twenty years. Dozens of American lawyers belong to an association that, free of charge, will defend a prisoner on a capital charge. The defence may take place either at the initial trial of the accused or in the later penalty phase, during which the same jury that convicted the prisoner hears arguments relating to the punishment they then recommend to the judge.

John Delgado, a high-powered 40-year-old attorney from South Carolina, and a member of this association, had joined George Turner, a local lawyer from Melbourne, Florida, for the defence of Russell Moore. Moore was an Australian Aboriginal, the son of Frank Whyman and Beverley Moore. Their son was born on 31 January 1963 in North Fitzroy. His grandmother, after being spoken to 'for some time' by officials from the Victorian Aborigines Welfare Board, agreed that 'it would be best if the baby were adopted'. Mrs Whyman, née Beverley Moore, fifteen years of age, signed the adoption consent, as required under the Victorian *Adoption of Children Act*, on 13 February 1963. Twelve days later, under a provision that enables relinquishing mothers to revoke their decision up to a month after signing the consent, Mrs Whyman rescinded her decision. She was then interviewed by members of the Welfare Board who 'pointed out to the girl that this did not necessarily mean that her baby would be returned to her as she seemed incapable of looking after it and had no suitable accommodation to which to take it'.

On 4 March 1963, the Reverend Graeme and Nesta Savage adopted Russell Moore and gave him the name James. In 1968, when Russell was five, he was taken to the United States by the Savages. When he was twelve his adoptive parents returned to Australia without him. For the next twelve years Moore lived on the streets and was convicted of various juvenile and criminal offences.[5] On 23 November 1988 he brutally killed Barbara Ann Barber, a prominent fashion designer of Melbourne, Florida, and a year later, pleading guilty, was convicted of first degree murder, robbery and sexual battery. The trial was short, since defence attorneys Delgado and Turner were planning to use the legal, historical and psychological arguments, which would have been used at this time in an Australian court, for the penalty phase, which was scheduled to begin a few weeks later on 11 December 1989.

I was brought up to date with these developments in Redfern at the beginning of December, when, discussing the case with some of Moore's relatives, I was informed that I had been asked by the Victorian Aboriginal Legal Service, whose client Moore had become, to travel to Florida as part of a team of Australians to testify on his behalf. My role would be to describe the system under which Moore had been removed from his family, and using my experiences as field-worker in the Aboriginal organisation Link-Up, to describe the traumas experienced by the removed children. We arrived on Saturday night, 36 hours before the penalty phase was to commence.

Some of the next day, Sunday, was spent conferring with Delgado about the particular expertise that each of us could bring to the defence. Here was a problem. Florida law allowed only evidence relating to the prisoner or his past life to be entered. None of us had met Russell Moore, and there was doubt about the legal relevance of the general history of the assimilation policy to Moore in particular. In the evening I was interviewed formally for an hour by the prosecution lawyers, testing my qualifications in advance of an appearance before the judge the next day. I learnt that this procedure allowed the opposing lawyers to prepare arguments against the status of witnesses or the extent of their evidence. Unused to interrogation by hostile lawyers, I had been unsettled by their unsmiling demeanour and relentless probing of my areas of weakness, particularly my lack of personal knowledge of Moore.

That sombre meeting on the Sunday night, the night before the penalty phase began, was followed by another. Delgado, summoning the dozen members of the Australian contingent together, announced his pessimistic opinion that though it might be possible to sway the jury to the lesser penalty of 25 imprisonment, the judge would probably over-rule that recommendation. Mrs Whyman had answered a reporter's insensitive question as to how she felt about the possibility of her son's execution, that she had blocked thinking about it. She felt that she was in the middle of the ocean, drowning. Delgado began to outline the Florida penalty phase procedures, which would begin the next morning. To a comment about the moral issues involved in capital punishment, he claimed passionately that to him it was a matter both of principle and of the personalities with whom he was involved. 'Just understand me, please. Bausch [the principal prosecution attorney] wants to kill Russell Moore. Think about that!' Turning to Mrs Whyman he declaimed: 'They want to do nothing but electrocute your son, lady. They want to take him out and fry him. Now I've already had to shake hands and say goodbye to one client I worked with for seven years . . . and . . . and . . .' His words fell into a horrified silence.

Delgado had reinforced something I had not yet fully appreciated. Death in the electric chair or life imprisonment were the only two possibilities of sentence. If we had travelled to Florida to dispute whether he was to spend twenty or 25 years in jail, we might have retained some of the 'friendly opposition' feeling found in Australian courts sometimes. But the prosecution lawyers wanted to execute Moore. Every question they asked, each objection they made, was intended to sway the jury, and later the judge, to that end alone. Their purpose lowered over us all during the five days I spent in Florida, and makes even the recollection of these events oppressive. The prosecution attorneys became almost physical enemies. It did not seem appropriate even to say good morning to them.

Florida Today announced on Monday morning that prosecution attorney Bausch had 'some very very strong problems' with his discovery that Delgado's star witness, Hal Wootten, the former Supreme Court Judge and New South Wales Commissioner into Aboriginal Deaths in Custody, had not met Russell Moore. To frustrate his obvious intended objection to Wootten's status as expert witness, it was clearly imperative that everyone who was to testify on his behalf meet and talk with him as soon as time could be found. That was not easy. Three of us who had not yet met him would probably be called that afternoon to the qualifying proceedings, in which the full court, without the jury, would consider whether, and about what, each of us would be allowed to give evidence to the jury.

My allotted share of Moore's time was twenty minutes of the lunch break of that Monday, which in addition I was to share with the Australian solicitor, who in turn was conducting a psychological test on the instructions of a Harvard psychiatrist giving evidence on Thursday. My visit to the prisoner, therefore, was not expected to produce any revelations. It seemed a legalistic rather than a useful manoeuvre, but whatever reservations I had about the plan I kept to myself: Ken Inglis had observed to me before I left Australia that academics often made the worst witnesses because they think they know better than lawyers. So I had determined to do what the lawyers thought best.

I was led to the cell below the court where Moore was held between the proceedings. It was a cream-coloured, dismal affair some two metres by three. There was a small bench, on which sat the solicitor and Moore, both looking out of place in their suits. There was a lidless and seatless aluminium toilet, nothing else. I was briefly introduced to Moore, then I squashed myself into what was left of the bench and tried to look inconspicuous.

'Do you consider yourself persecuted?' intoned the solicitor.
'Yeah,' replied Moore emphatically.
'Do you like to write poetry?'
'No.'
'Do you tell things to your mother and father?'
'Well, I haven't got a father. He's dead.'

Since Moore's natural father, Frank Whyman, had died many years ago, and his adopting father, Graeme Savage, was upstairs half-way through lunch at that moment, I thought his denial significant. The questions droned on. Some seemed to my untrained ear to be silly or boring: perhaps they were the check questions built into the assessment. So I switched off my concentration and tried to 'feel the vibes', by absorbing impressions of Moore's face, accent and demeanour as well as his answers.

When the court convened, Commissioner Wootten took the stand for the qualifying session. Naturally, witnesses due to appear later were not allowed to enter the room, but it was possible to get an idea of what was happening by listening to the proceedings over the headphones of the television crews outside. At 4.15 their shouted exclamations indicated that something dramatic had happened inside. A babble of voices from the people emerging made it clear: the judge had ruled that Wootten, though eminently well qualified in law, was unqualified to speak on the legally allowable matters. He would not allow Wootten to speak in general terms about the forced assimilation of Aboriginal children. Delgado and Wootten pushed through the crowd to where the Australian supporters were gathered. Wootten stood aside while Delgado, surrounded by cameras, lights and a dozen shouting press people, tried to make the best of what was obviously a bad situation. The significance of the decision was not lost upon the prospective witnesses either: besides Wootten, there were half a dozen of us who had come from Australia to give similar evidence.

After tea it was my turn. The jury remained out. For an hour and a quarter I was led, mostly by the prosecution lawyers, through my knowledge of south-eastern Australian Aboriginal history. Most disconcerting were their efforts to find out what I thought of Moore, and by what means I had arrived at my appraisal. The purpose of my brief visit to the cell sounded as manufactured as undoubtedly it was. The lawyers asked me what Moore's answers were to the questions I had heard. I looked at Delgado for help. Neither he nor Moore looked perturbed. Well, I was there to help the prisoner and my immediate purpose was to avoid Wootten's fate. I had to get myself qualified to speak to the jury the following day. If such help as I could give meant a serious breach of social-worker ethics, so be it. I began to describe the questions and answers I had heard and wished I had paid more attention to them in the last ten minutes of my visit.

In the end the prosecution lawyers offered no objection to my status as a witness qualified to speak, as the judge defined it, on 'Aboriginal history and Aborigine culture'; though I was specifically enjoined not to mention an estimate of 15,000 Koori children having been removed from south-eastern Australia. The emotive and technically irrelevant fact, it was held, might influence the jury to consider matters other than Moore's immediate and past life.

The fate of Wootten caused Delgado to reason that I and an Australian psychologist should speak to Moore again before our appearance before the jury next morning. That evening we arrived at the Brevard County jail, where followed a good deal of argument about my status and visiting rights from the not unfriendly jail staff. Only a late phone call from the judge himself ensured my admission to see Moore after 9 pm.

Moore still had no idea who I was, but I suppose that he has seen hundreds of people like me staring at him, trying to win his confidence, through the armoured glass of the meeting room. From my years as a Link-Up worker I have learnt to approach prisoners as any other clients, that is to talk about my own life, and about Link-Up, for a few minutes before asking any questions. But Moore was neither surly nor reticent. I think he was on a high from having just spoken to the psychologist for nearly an hour. He confidently showed me psychologists', doctors' and other officials' reports about his behaviour in jail. In the course of what I hoped was rather more of a conversation than an interrogation, I asked him who he thought was persecuting him. 'Why, the governor [of the jail] is out to get me.'

I left the jail after 50 minutes with the strong impression that while Moore was intelligent enough to know the right answers to certain questions and propositions, asked many times by the prison psychologists, he did not know what to make about all the talk of the previous three months about Victorian Aborigines, about his real family, about his mother's love, about an Aboriginal identity and about the assimilation policy. The information was so strange, and the feelings of love and brotherhood from his family were so strong, that he was simply at a loss to know what the correct responses were to satisfy the psychiatrists. The enormous change in Aboriginal self-perceptions about their history that has taken place in the last twenty years had bypassed him completely: three months before, for all he knew, he could have been the last Aborigine born in Australia. He had never associated with black people, Australian or American, at any time of his life.

I went to bed that night at about 8 am Australian time and spent a terrible night. Jet-lagged, and conscious of a considerable responsibility on me not just to tell the story accurately but to tell it in a way most likely to sway the jury, I woke at about 4.30 American time, and paced up and down my room rehearsing what I hoped would appear to be the spontaneous answers to questions I had already been given by Delgado. Was Moore's removal related to a larger Australian policy of removal? What behavioural characteristics were likely to flow from trans-cultural adoptions? In what way was Moore like other removed Aborigines that I had worked with?

I practised my answer to Delgado's question about any options Mrs Whyman might have retained. I would reply that the conversation the welfare authorities had with her after she revoked her consent was revealing: 'Beverley was told that if she returned to Deniliquin either with or without the baby she would be inviting police action against herself and Frank.' The reference to Frank Whyman was a not very subtle threat of a carnal knowledge charge. The threat to herself undoubtedly was the charge of being an uncontrolled minor, which would render her liable to removal to an institution, whereupon Russell would be declared to be a potentially or actually neglected child, and removed to a babies home as a State Ward.

Delgado was then to ask: Were there any alternatives to adopting Russell? Yes, I would reply: To Aboriginal people, a child who is well loved is by definition well cared for. If in the first instance Mrs Whyman had been unable to care for Russell, the next step should have been to invite her extended family to find a home for him; failing that, within the Victorian Aboriginal community; failing that, Russell could have been declared a State Ward and sent to a foster home. Adoption should have been the last alternative. Yet the Welfare Board officials had chosen adoption first. There was no evidence that they had ever considered other alternatives.

I then planned to explain to the jury what would have happened to Moore if, instead, he had been sent to an institution like the Orana Methodist Children's Home. At the time of his birth, that institution was midway between the old-fashioned congregate care, of large dormitories and communal mess hall, and the modern concept of family group homes of four or five children scattered in the suburbs. The 1963 style was half a dozen family homes of ten children and a house parent scattered in the grounds of the institution. Unlike adopted children, foster children could be visited by their parents. Nor was there prohibition against their returning to parental care if the Minister of Child Welfare was satisfied that it was in the child's best interests. Why, then, was Moore not sent there? For two reasons; one was that Orana's council was unsure of the wisdom of removing Aboriginal children from their families; another was that the authorities were in duty bound, by their own *Aborigines Welfare Act*, to adopt him.

At this point I planned a short explanation of the *Victorian Adoption Act* of 1928. In the 35 years to 1963, the most significant amendment to it was that which allowed Mrs Whyman a month in which to revoke her Consent to

Adoption. Under the Act, the effect of consent to adoption was 'permanently to deprive' natural parents of their parental rights: 'Upon an adoption order being made, all rights, duties, obligations and liabilities of the parent or parents . . . in relation to the future custody, maintenance and education of the adopted child, including all rights to appoint a guardian, or the consent to marriage shall be extinguished.'

The point of adoption was that the child became not only legally but also, as it were, physically the child of the new parents. A few anomalies remained. The child in law retained both Birth Certificates, the original as well as the new one, but was allowed access only to the latter. Another exception to the process of 'rebirthing' was that the child could inherit property from a natural parent. A further complication, unrecognised at the time, was that a child adopted to foreign nationals probably retained its Australian citizenship if it was removed overseas by those parents. Apart from these minor though confusing exceptions, the spirit of the Adoption Act was clear. Legally, emotionally and physically, the natural parents were deemed not so much to have ceased to exist, but never to have existed at all. The child would not be interested in its real identity, because it would not know that it ever had another one.

There are no figures for the number of Victorian Aboriginal children removed from their parents' care and placed with white parents. Nor are there figures available for the number of children adopted in contrast to other forms of substitute care. However, it is worth noting several significant differences between the Aboriginal administrations in New South Wales and Victoria. First, Victoria did not have institutions designed specially for Aboriginal children. There was no equivalent of the Cootamundra or Kinchela homes of New South Wales. A second difference was that the Victorian administration, at the time Moore was born, was itself only six years old. It had come into existence for one purpose:

> It shall be the function of the Board to promote the moral, intellectual and physical welfare of aborigines . . . with a view to their assimilation into the general community.

The new Victorian Board was under much pressure to perform. All forms of separation except adoption allowed the possibility of natural family ties being retained, or later rejoined. Most institutions encouraged it. 'So ladies and gentlemen of the jury,' I practised repeatedly, 'that is why Russell Moore was adopted, even though Mrs Whyman and her extended family were able to take care of Russell.' By definition, the Aborigines Welfare Board was established to assimilate Aborigines. By convention, adoption was the most permanent method of securing assimilation. By law, therefore, the authorities had to adopt him because any other procedure would have been in defiance of the Board's own Act and the government's wishes. That was why Moore was adopted when he was eight weeks old. The intention was that he should never learn his real identity.

Granted, therefore, that it was not just the officials' but the government's intention to assimilate Moore—was adoption in his personal best interest? First I planned to concede that in certain circumstances adoption of white children by white parents had advantages. For all the grief and cruelty undoubtedly caused to many relinquishing mothers, I would argue that the principle of a child being unaware that it has been adopted and raised by a loving family, was not altogether a bad one from the child's viewpoint. Often it worked. But Moore was, and is, very dark and distinctly Koori in appearance. He could not possibly have imagined that he was the Savages' real child.

So the argument over cross-racial adoptions, where it is

apparent that children are not biological offspring, is altogether different from one where adopted children look like the new parents and are unaware of their history. This is particularly so in the case of Aboriginal children adopted by white parents, in which the ambience of society, whatever the love bestowed, or not bestowed, by the adopting parents, is hostile towards Aboriginality. An analysis of the clients seeking assistance from the Victorian Aboriginal Legal Service for criminal charges has shown that 90 per cent have been in foster, institutional or adoptive placement. There was a sharp distinction between what the law required and what was in Moore's best interests.

At this point I expected an objection under cross-examination: surely the knowledge of the detrimental effects of cross-racial adoption was not available at the time? My answer to this expected question from the prosecution was to be: yes, or at the least, the information was there but disregarded. I had not had the opportunity to study the Victorian case histories of removed Aborigines, but as a Link-Up caseworker in New South Wales I had studied over a thousand case histories of the 10,000 Aboriginal children removed from their parents in New South Wales. Quite simply, they are horrifying. I did not expect to be allowed to cite any of the histories of people who went insane, spent their entire lives in institutions, died of disease, committed a variety of violent acts including murder and suicide, abandoned their own children, were rendered incapable of forming stable relationships, or who, at the end of the period of separation, but now traumatised for life, went back as adults to the missions and camps. My own study of Wiradjuri children, taken from southern-central New South Wales, revealed that, according to the Board's own records, 70 girls were removed between 1916 and 1928. Ten unmarried girls fell pregnant to whites— so much for the argument about the moral danger of the camps. Ten spent periods in mental hospitals, and seven died. Out of a combined total of 84 boys and girls, between half and three quarters of the children eventually returned home. In New South Wales the psychological damage the children suffered could not even be justified by the criterion of assimilation. The policy was not only cruel, but useless.

Adoptions were different. Far fewer adoptees found their own way home, because they often did not know who they were or where they were from, and they had adoptive relatives who generally took a close interest in dissuading them from returning. Australian society remained deeply inimical to Aborigines, whether they behaved like whites or not. Russell Moore would have found it very difficult to obtain a white-collar job, no matter what clothes he arrived in for an interview. He could expect trouble from the police, whatever his actions; his presence in a hotel would be liable to challenge; he would be lucky to join a golf club or get a bank loan. Neither a suit, an accent nor a stable personality built on love and respect in the home would make a twenty-year-old Aboriginal man acceptable to much white society outside the charmed family circle.

Family love could not protect the child, or the adult, away from that circle. When at school the children were called 'a black cunt' or 'a dirty abo', adopting parents could provide no relief beyond 'Just ignore it.' It was common in many adoptive homes for every reference to homeless, arrested or demonstrating Aborigines in the papers or television to be accompanied by the injunction 'Don't be like them.' In the homes of children who had not been removed, there was security in phrases like 'just keep away from them fucking gubs'. That antagonistic group identity had enabled the Kooris to survive as self-identifying Indigenous people, but it was an identity that Moore never shared. It was not an accident that he had not associated with black people in all his life. Very few adopted children, in my experience, have done so during adolescence.

What, then, might have been the course of Moore's life if he had been declared a State Ward, placed in foster care, and remained in Australia? He might well have quarrelled with his foster parents before the age of twelve, and might have run away from home once or twice before he was fifteen. He might have come under minor police notice in a gang of white youths for breaking and entering and car thefts. By the age of eighteen he might well have spent time in a reformatory. On release, he very probably would have come to Melbourne in search of work and adventure, having by now abandoned his foster family permanently. There, having met other Aborigines in reform schools, he might have made his way to the Victorian Aboriginal Child Care Service, which offers a similar service to Link-Up in New South Wales. But if he was still unsure or ashamed of his Aboriginal identity, it is highly probably that a scene similar to this would have taken place. While Moore was drinking alone in a pub, another Aboriginal would have approached him:

'Hey, brother, what's your country?'

'Australia.'

'Eh? No, cuz, where was you born?'

'Sea Lake.'

'Oh yeah, Who's your family?'

'Eh?'

'What's your name?'

'James Savage.'

'That's not a Koori name.'

'No, I'm adopted.'

'What's your real name?'

'I don't know.'

'Well you wanna get home and find your people. Don't

wanna be too flash. You look like a Whyman to me.
Shake hands. I'm your cousin.'

Those unfamiliar with southern Koori society might be
surprised at how quickly I have allowed Moore to be identified in this imaginary scene. But the Victorian community is
not large. Russell Moore looks so much like his mother that
I am certain he would have been identified as her missing
son before he was twenty. Shortly after this scene, at the age
of seventeen or eighteen, he would have gone home to a
joyful reunion with his mother and siblings.

Joyful—at first. After ten years, the Link-Up staff know
that the first meeting with the natural family is not the end,
but the beginning of a long and difficult journey. It might
have been some time before Russell called Mrs Whyman
'Mum'. Perhaps he never would have become as proud and
as confident of his identity as the other family members. But
he would have been looked after. There was a home established for young people with problems like his, managed by
the same person who travelled with us as an expert witness
on the effects of separation. If he was sick, he would have
gone to the Aboriginal Medical Service. If he ran foul of the
law, he would have been counselled by an Aboriginal field-
worker in the Aboriginal Legal Service and represented by
an Aboriginal Legal Service lawyer. If he went to jail, he
would have found Aboriginal prisoners to protect him and
been counselled by an Aboriginal jail worker. These forms of
protection were the adult equivalent of that antagonistic
group identity Moore did not receive as a child. Aboriginal
people have looked for help not among sympathetic whites
but among themselves. They alone know what it is like to
live in a country infested with white faces.

I did not expect to be able to say all this to the jury, but
I had prepared my thoughts in case the prosecution was

napping. By daybreak the arguments were securely, I hoped, in my head. By 7 am, as arranged, I was at the café across the road from the Dixie Motel, breakfasting on coffee and sugary doughnuts with John Delgado while he again rehearsed the questions (but not the answers). By 7.20 he was gone to have another breakfast with another of the day's witnesses.

At 8.00 am I was outside the courtroom, nervously placing the floor. Molly Dyer, who established the first Victorian services to help removed Aboriginal children, entered first. She emerged an hour later, having with grace and dignity placed Moore in the perspective of psychological damage that he and other Aboriginal children had suffered by removal. But simultaneously Delgado emerged, looking worried and uttering 'damn damn damn' under his breath.

I never did find out how he had come by the information that the prosecution was preparing to put to me, on the basis of my previous testimony, the question: 'Dr Read, you say that under certain circumstances adopted Aboriginal children have a tendency towards violence or self-destruction. But are you aware that James Savage [they insisted on calling him by his adopted name] has committed over fifteen serious crimes, including armed robbery and sexual assault?' My answer would have been no, since I had made it my business, on advice, to know as little as possible of such matters. Delgado would then have instantly, and correctly, objected that the prisoner's previous convictions were inadmissible evidence. But by then it would have been too late. The jury members, having heard the disallowed question, would not then be able to put the information out of their minds. None of the evidence I was about to give, nor that of the psychologist, nor that of the Aboriginal Teenage Home manager, would, in Delgado's view, be sufficient to counteract that one sentence of inadmissible evidence. At the last minute, therefore, we were all withdrawn as expert witnesses for the defence.

Though it was only 10.30 on Wednesday, this development brought legal proceedings to the end for the day. There was still a slight possibility that we might be called the next day, which meant that we could not be present when the person now billed as the star defence witness, the top-ranking Harvard psychologist who had asked that the psychological assessment be carried out, was due to testify that Moore was so psychologically damaged as to be incapable of taking responsibility for his actions.

Friday was the day, the judge had ordered, when the hearing must be concluded. It was the first time I had been in the court while the jury was sitting. I listened to the prosecution's attempt to allow Graeme Savage to deny that he had beaten Russell as a child. Emotionally, he testified that in California in the early 1970s he had tried to establish an integrated church. So vehement was the resistance of the Californian whites that he and Mrs Savage had received death threats. In a six-month period he was so distressed by the campaign against him that he did not remember what, if anything, he had done to his adopted son.

The summing-up that followed this last witness was low-key. The prosecution, contrary to Delgado's expectation, did not show the video of the murder scene and victim, nor produce the murder weapon, to reinforce the brutality of the crime. In deference to local southern opinion, it was not Delgado but George Turner, the local lawyer, who summed up the defence's case. The jury adjourned. We went for lunch at a local takeaway, where I accidentally encountered some members of the Savage family. They did not look pleased to see me, but I had been moved by Graeme Savage's testimony that morning. His distress seemed genuine. Few white Australians guessed at the depth and intensity of commonplace white antipathy towards Aborigines in the 1960s.

The jury emerged to ask about the exact meaning of 'life

sentence', a question taken to be a promising sign by the Australians. They retired for another half an hour, then emerged to an atmosphere of extreme tension. We arranged ourselves as Delgado had suggested: black Australians sitting at the front behind Moore, other supporters on the same side at the back. As the official handed the judge the verdict I grabbed the hand of an Australian sitting beside me, and must have held it tightly for the whole of the long ten seconds it took for him to read out the majority decision of life imprisonment—25 calendar years.

When it was over, the media descended upon Mrs Whyman and the defence team. I wanted a few minutes of quiet, so I walked out down the corridor, which overlooked the car park. After ten minutes I saw her, in the fading winter light, escorted by friends, fighting her way to her car. The bright lights of the clamouring media still surrounded her, spot-lit literally and figuratively as she had been for three months. It is the clearest visual memory I have of the whole trial. It was a painful ordeal for her, and I reflected on how much more painful it would have been if the jury had awarded the death sentence.

The same thought was in my mind five weeks later, when on 23 January 1990 the judge announced that he had overridden the jury's eleven-to-one decision and had imposed the death penalty. Two factors had helped him influence his decision, he said. One was the large majority of mail he had received in favour of death. The other was that he believed Moore's previous unhappy history did not account to a mitigating circumstance; many people, including survivors of concentration camps, had emerged to lead useful lives.

There was speculation that the verdict had been framed more with an eye to the judge's subsequent re-election than to the reasons he outlined. But I thought the judgment, though disappointing, predictable in the Florida context.

Arguably, judges ought to take community feelings into account, while noting whether any sections of it are under-represented or over-represented. Moore's crime was a terrible one: I imagine many black men have been executed in Florida for less brutal murders. Perhaps the law implicitly recognises that society maintains its stability by keeping at arm's length such pleas as diminished responsibility.

The position now is that the judge's sentence is reviewed automatically by the Florida Supreme Court, which in recent years has overturned all but one of the death sentences that have been imposed against the recommendations of the jury. The Minister of Aboriginal Affairs believed, in that event, special circumstances might warrant an exception to the rule that Australians are not returned to Australia to serve sentences imposed in other countries. It would be necessary to conclude either an international agreement with the United States or a specific agreement concerning Moore alone. The agreement of the Victoria or other state government responsible for an appropriate prison would also be necessary.

The responsibility of the Commonwealth and the states in the mean time is to recognise that Aboriginal childcare is an Aboriginal responsibility, to change the adoption laws in states that have not already done so to ensure that Aboriginal adoptees can find out who they really are, and to fund the Link-Up work sufficiently in all states. It may be too late to help Moore, but it is not too late to help the thousands of removed children who have not found a place in white or black Australian society, who remain, at this minute, at the edge of the firelight, frightened, or aggressive, or hating, or yearning, or frustrated, or aching to be loved, or forgetting, or forgotten.

Bibliography

ABM [Australian Board of Missions] Review

Abo Call (newspaper)

Aborigines Welfare Board, *Dawn* (monthly journal)

Archives Office of NSW, Aborigines Protection/Welfare Board
    Annual Reports, 1921–22, 1926–27
    Copies of Letters Sent
    Register of Wards 1916–1928

Australia, Senate 1974 *Senate Select Committee Report on Environmental Conditions of Aborigines 1971–76*, AGPS, Canberra 59 of 1974

Barwick, D.E. 1972, 'Coranderrk and Cumeroogunga: pioneers and policy', in T. Scarlett Epstein and D.H. Penny eds, *Opportunity and Response: Case Studies in Economic Development*, London

Berndt, R.M. and C.H. Berndt 1951, 'An Oenpelli monologue', *Oceania*, XXII/I (Sept)

Biskup, P. 1973, *Not Slaves Not Citizens*, QUP, St Lucia

Bowden, R. and B. Bunbury eds 1990, *Being Aboriginal* Australian Broadcasting Corporation, Crows Nest

Commonwealth of Australia 1937, 'Initial conference of Commonwealth and State Aboriginal Authorities', Government Printer, Canberra

Cummings, B. *Take This Child*, 1990 Aboriginal Studies Press, Canberra

Curthoys, A. 1997, 'Entangled histories: Conflict and Ambivalence in non-Aboriginal Australia', in G. Gray and C. Winter, eds, *The Resurgence of Racism*, Monash Publications in History, Clayton, pp. 117–28

Davis, J. 1985, 'Urban Aboriginal', in K. Gilbert ed. 1985, *Inside Black Australia*, Penguin, Ringwood

Eckermann, A-K. 1973, 'Group Identity and Urban Aborigines' in D. Tugby ed. *Aboriginal Identification in Contemporary Australian Society*, AIAS, Canberra

Edwards, C. 1982, 'Is The Ward Clean?', in B. Gammage and A. Markus eds, *All That Dirt*, History Project Inc., Canberra pp. 4–8

——1989, *It's a Long Road Back* (film) AIAS

Edwards, C. and P. Read eds 1986 'The Yearning of My Soul, Accounts of Journeys to Aboriginal Identity', typescript in the possession of the author

——1989, *The Lost Children*, Doubleday, Sydney

General Assembly of the United Nations 1949, *Universal Declaration of Human Rights*, Geneva

Gilbert, K. ed. 1973, *Living Black*, Penguin, Ringwood

——ed. 1988, *Inside Black Australia*, Penguin, Ringwood

Goodall, H. 1996, *Invasion to Embassy*, Allen & Unwin, Sydney

Gungil Jindibah Centre 1994, 'Learning from the Past, Aboriginal Perspectives on the Effects and Implications of Welfare Policies and Practices on Aboriginal Families in New South Wales', Lismore

Haebich, A. 1988, *For Their Own Good*, UWA Press, Perth

Horton, D. (General Editor) 1994, *The Encyclopaedia of Aboriginal Australia*, Aboriginal Studies Press, Canberra

Human Rights and Equal Opportunity Commission 1997, 'Bringing Them Home', HREOC, Sydney

Jupp, J. ed. 1988, *The Australian People*, Angus and Robertson, Ryde

Kidd, R. 1977, 'Regulating Bodies: Administrations and Aborigines in Queensland: 1840–1988', unpublished thesis cited in HREOC

Lake, M. 1998, 'Feminism and the Gendered Politics of Antiracism, Australia 1927–57: From Maternal Protectionism to Leftist Assimilation', in *Australian Historical Studies*, 110 (April 1998) pp. 91–108

Langton, M. 1981, 'Urbanising Aborigines—The Social Scientists' Great Deception', in *Social Alternatives* 2/2 (August 1981), pp. 16–22

Link-Up (QLD) Aboriginal Corporation 1991, 'Link-Up', Brisbane

Maastricht Human Rights Project Group 1992, University of Limburgh, 'Seminar on the right to restitution, compensation and rehabilitation for victims of gross violations of human rights and fundamental freedoms', Netherlands Institute for Human Rights, The Hague

MacDonald, R. and Australian Archives 1985, *Between Two Worlds*, IAD Press, Alice Springs

Manne, R. 1998, 'The Stolen Generations', *Quadrant* (Jan–Feb)

Marcus, A. 1990, *Governing Savages*, Allen & Unwin, North Sydney

Maris, H. and S. Borg 1985, *Women of the Sun*, Penguin, Ringwood

Mattingley, C. and K. Hampton eds 1988, *Survival in Our Own Land*, Wakefield Press, Adelaide

McLeod, P. 1989, 'The yearning of my soul', poster

Minister for Aboriginal Affairs 1997, Press Statement, 16 December

Mongta, A. 1982, 'Perspective of the Aboriginal Child in Substitute Care', Principal Report II, FACSA, roneo

New South Wales Parliament 1967, 'Report From the Joint Committee into Aborigines Welfare', II, Minutes of Evidence

O'Connor, L. 1998, 'The more things change', (history thesis, University of Sydney) published in J. Kociumbas ed. *Maps Dreams History*, Sydney Studies in History, University of Sydney, 1998

Partington, G. 1996, *Hasluck versus Coombs*, Quakers Hill Press, Sydney

Perkins, C. 1975, *A Bastard Like Me*, Ure Smith, Sydney

Randall, R. 1986, *Bob Randall*, CAAMA, Alice Springs (cassette tape)

Read, P. ed. 1978–89, *A Social History of the Northern Territory*, 9 part series, Government Printer Northern Territory, Canberra

——1981, 'The Stolen Generations', New South Wales Government Printer, Sydney

——1983, 'Link-Up', Link-Up (NSW) Aboriginal Corporation, Canberra

——ed. 1984, *Down There With Me on the Cowra Mission*, Pergamon, Sydney

——1987, 'The two journeys of Dianne Westmacott', *Aboriginal History*, 11, pp. 82–90

——1988, *A Hundred Years War*, ANU Press, Canberra

——1990, *Charles Perkins A Biography*, Viking, Ringwood

——1990a, 'In the Middle of the Ocean, Drowning', *Overland*, 119 (1990), pp. 54–62

——1992, 'A phantom at my shoulder. Writing the last draft of *Charles Perkins a biography*, in I. Donaldson, P. Read and J. Walter eds *Shaping Lives*, Humanities Research Centre, Canberra, pp. 155–170

——1996, 'Report on Records Produced by Subpoena', typescript

——1996a, 'Reparation for Victims of Separation', in ATSIC, 'Submission to the Human Rights and Equal Opportunity Commission into the Separation of Aboriginal Islander Children . . .', Appendix C, pp. 39–42, Canberra

——1997, 'Submission to the National Enquiry into the Separation of Aboriginal and Torres Strait Islander Children from their Families', typescript Canberra

——1998, 'Bringing Them Home', *Mots pluriels*, electronic journal

Read, P. and J. Read 1992, *Long Time Olden Time: Aboriginal Accounts of Northern Territory History*, Institute for Aboriginal Development, Alice Springs

——1993, *Long Time Olden Time*, CD Rom, Firmware, Penrith

Roach, A. 1990, *Charcoal Lane*, CD, Mushroom Records

Rose, M. 1996, *For The Record*, Allen & Unwin, Sydney

Summerlad, E. 1976, 'Homes for Blacks: Aboriginal Community and Adoption, in C. Picton ed. 1976, *Proceedings of the First Australian Conference on Adoption*, February 1976, Committee of the First Australian Conference on Adoption, UNSW, Kensington

Tucker, M. 1977, *If Everybody Cared*, Angus & Robertson, Sydney

Van Boven 1993, 'Study concerning the right to restitution . . .', final report by special rapporteur, UN Sub-Commission on Prevention of Discrimination and Protection of Minorities

Wootten, H. QC 1989, 'Report of the Inquiry into the Death of Malcolm Charles Smith', AGPS Perth

——1990, 'Report of the Inquiry into the Death of Clarence Alec Nean', Royal Commission into Aboriginal Deaths in Custody, AGPS, Perth

Endnotes

Prologue The Stolen Generations: Who are we?

1   In May 1995 the Federal Labor government directed the Human Rights and Equal Opportunity Commission to investigate the separation of Aboriginal children from their parents. Just before the enquiry began I was asked to write a page to add to the information being handed out at the official opening of the enquiry. It was politely rejected as being a bit over the top. I suspect that if the function organisers knew then what they were to learn by the end of the enquiry, the piece would have been accepted.

2   '7.30 Report', ABC, October 1998

Chapter 1   The oral evidence

1   Veronica Cameron's interview, recorded in 1976, was first published in 'The Mission Stations' vol. 8 of P. Read 1978–89, p. 16. The interview with Topsy Nelson Napurrula was published in Read and Read 1992 based on an interview made in 1977.

The interview with Joy Williams was published in Edwards and Read 1989, pp. 49–54. The Aileen Wedge interview appeared in Read 1984, pp. 100–6.

Chapter 2 The written evidence

1   Most of this chapter is based on a personal submission I made to the Stolen Generations enquiry in 1996 entitled 'The removal of Aboriginal children and their subsequent history, with special reference to the Wiradjuri people of New South Wales'. The story of the missionaries in the Wellington Valley is adapted from Read 1988, pp. 16–19.

2   Initial conference of Commonwealth and state Aboriginal authorities, Canberra, April 1937, p. 3; Read 1990, p. 10.

3   Mr Flowers, in New South Wales Parliamentary Debates, 1914–15 (Legislative Assembly), pp. 1353–4.

4   J. Gray, quoted in C. Mattingley and K. Hampton 1988, p. 160.

5   At this time Tasmania refused to concede that any Aborigines survived in the state, and therefore established no Aboriginal-specific legislation or institutions. Victoria had no state-run Aboriginal homes either, its statutory authority apparently preferring to send the separated children away to many different institutions.

6   Haebich 1988, p. 182.

7   Hagar Roberts, in Read and Read 1992, p. 101; see also Berndt and Berndt 1951, pp. 28–30.

8   NSW Aborigines Protection Board, Annual Report, 1911.

9   Randall 1985.

10 Edwards and Read, p. ix.

11 Read 1981, p. 9.

12 Pers. comm., officer of the NSW Dept of Youth and Community Services, June, 1986.

13 NSW *Aborigines Protection Act*, No 25 of 1909, s 13a.

14 Mr Flowers, in New South Wales Parliamentary Debates, 1914–15, (LA), pp. 1353–4.
15 NSW Acts of Parliament, No 2 of 1915, s 2 (I) (a).
16 'Initial conference of Commonwealth and state Aboriginal Authorities 1937, p. 3.
17 Amendment No 12 of 1940, No 3 (b) (1).
18 NSW *Children (Care and Protection) Act*, No 54 of 1987, s 87.
19 P. Coe in Read 1984, pp. 90–4; family interviews.
20 Mrs I. Edwards, 1992, interview transcript in Griffith City Library.
21 Mrs F. Doolan, in Read 1984, p. 117.
22 Survey Result in APB General Correspondence, State Archives of NSW, box 8/2884.
23 Interview by C. Edwards, 9 February 1980.
24 A. Adams in Edwards and Read, pp. 45–6.
25 Edwards 1989 (Soundtrack of film).
26 Pers. comm, by a former Kinchela inmate, now deceased.
27 Evidence of J. White, Manager, 8 May 1962, during an Aborigines Welfare Board enquiry into alleged sexual perversion at the Home, APB General Correspondence, box 8/2995.
28 Wootten 1990, pp. 42–6.
29 Evidence J. Henricksen, NSW Parliament, Report from the joint committee into Aborigines welfare, 1967, vol. II, pp. 404–11.
30 Richard Murray in Read 1984, p. 98.
31 This and the following quotations are drawn from Edwards and Read.
32 Mongta 1982, pp. 43–4.
33 Summerlad 1976.
34 For example, the Northern Territory's 'two kilometre law' (*Summary Offences Act 1983*, s 45D) prohibited the consumption of alcohol in a public place within a defined distance from a liquor outlet. Though Aboriginal people were not specifically named, the intention to 'clean up' the streets of Northern Territory towns was perfectly clear.

35 A. Roach 1991.
36 Wootten 1989.
37 Davis in Gilbert 1988, p. 57.

Chapter 3 The Stolen Generations

1   In the early 1980s I used to visit a small state government research agency in Sydney called the Family and Children's Service Agency, established to reduce the high numbers of Aboriginal children living in non-Aboriginal care, and to prevent Aboriginal children being removed from their families and communities. In 1981 Chris Milne the director asked me to write an article setting the historical context of separation. A paper called 'The Stolen Generations' was the result. It circulated in a xeroxed form for a couple of months, then the state government published it as a pamphlet for mass circulation.

2   An Aboriginal station had a manager; an Aboriginal Reserve was unmanaged.

3   The Aborigines Protection (later Welfare) Board was established by the New South Wales government in 1883. The Aborigines Welfare Board was abolished in 1969.

4   *The Register of Wards 1916–1928*, like other records of the Aborigines Protection Board, is held at the Archives Office of New South Wales, Harrington Street, Sydney.

Chapter 4 'Like being born all over again': The establishment of Link-Up

1   This chapter is based on a booklet I wrote in 1984 with Coral Edwards' help for prospective clients of 'Link-Up' which drew on my new understanding of the records and my conversations

with many removed individuals. It was structured to answer the most frequently asked questions we had encountered.

2   Maris and Borg 1985.

3   In July 1984 this woman finally met her people for the first time in her life. She was 74.

Chapter 5 'I don't mix with Aboriginals you know': working with Link-Up clients

1   The story of 'Jane King' first appeared in Read 1988, pp. 66–70.

2   The second part of this chapter is based on the case history of 'Dianne Westmacott', who in 1983 approached Link-Up for assistance in finding her family and identity. The information is drawn from the files and from a recorded conversation with Ms Westmacott (Sydney, February 1987). I wrote the story following the sudden death of Dr Diane Barwick, a founder of the journal *Aboriginal History*, whose knowledge of Victorian Koori history helped us to locate the family of Dianne Westmacott. To protect the identity of both the adoptive and natural families, surnames were changed or omitted in the original published article. It was published in Read 1987.

3   Until 1969, two New South Wales state government authorities were charged with the care and protection of Aboriginal children: the Aborigines Welfare Board and the Department of Child Welfare. Children who were sent to the Aboriginal homes at Cootamundra and Kinchela were in the care of the Board; most others fell under the jurisdiction of the Child Welfare Department, which also handled all adoptions.

     Instructions that adopted children should be told of their status were not given until the mid-1970s, but parents were at no time advised to tell their children that they were of Aboriginal descent. Since 1982 it has been departmental policy, where possible, to place Aboriginal wards with Aboriginal foster parents.

4   Children might be removed from their parents in two ways: first by charging them with 'neglect' (in effect, with being neglected), second by charging them with 'being uncontrollable'. If the first charge was found proven, a child was likely to be declared a State Ward, for foster or adoptive placement; if the second, the placement was more likely to be a reformatory. In both cases, unless adopted, a child remained in the nominal care of the Minister for Child Welfare.

5   It is not clear how Colin Donaghue managed to do this. Perhaps he saw the adoption order held by Mr Westmacott (certificates at that time named the natural parents). The secret of natural identity was very jealously guarded by state authorities. Though most states now allow adopted adults to view their natural birth certificates at the age of eighteen, in 1981 no decision had been made in New South Wales. Normally adoptees had to ask the Adoptions Branch for special consideration to have contact made with the natural parents. If a favourable decision were taken by the Branch, it might even then be more than a year before contact were made. Then as now, it was possible that the natural parents might not want to see the child.

6   Barwick 1972, pp. 10–68.

7   Barwick 1972.

Chapter 6   At the edge of the firelight: coming home, partly

1   The first part of this chapter is drawn from Read 1990, ch. 3. The second comes from Read 1992, pp. 155–70. In the latter article I was trying to consider further Charles' changing attitudes to his institutionalisation, and more generally—the extra psychological burden carried today by adults like him who

were raised not by sadists and misfits, but by carers who genuinely loved their charges. This second extract begins at the point where I was discussing this issue.

2   C. Perkins recorded interview, tape 1.

3   C. Perkins tape 2, interview.

4   J. Moriarty, G. Briscoe 1, C. Perkins 2, interviews.

5   C. Perkins 2, G. Briscoe, W. Espie, interviews; Anglican Diocese of NT, roneoed notes, November 1982, 'Percy McDonald Smith: 1903–1982'.

6   W. Espie, J. Moriarty, C. Perkins 2.

7   W. Espie, G. Briscoe, C. Perkins 2.

8   J. Ferrier, Secretary for Aborigines, ABM, to Secretary of Interior, 17/12/1946, Australian Archives AANT 1070, F1 52/250.

9   C. Perkins, Curriculum Vitae; 'St Francis House for inland children, Semaphore, South Australia', Report 1947–48, ABM *Review*, xxvi (ll), 1/11/48, pp. 169.

10   C. Perkins 3; Percy Smith, interviewed in BBC film *Six Australians*, c.1967.

11   Interviews with J. Hill, J. Moriarty, V. Copley.

12   Interview with W. Espie.

13   W. Espie, W. Turner, C. Perkins, interviews.

14   C. Perkins 2, W. Espie

15   W. Espie, C. Perkins 3, G. Hill, G. Briscoe.

16   Espie recalls Smith expressing his regret to the assembled ex-St Francis boys at a reunion in the 1970s, ABM *Review*, xxvi (8), p. 170

17   'Field Survey: the Half Caste', ABM *Review*, xi/2, 1/2/1952: 21–2; R.K. McCaffery to Administrator, 3/2/1954, 'Coloured Children—policy': 6–7; AANT CA 1070, F1 52/250c.

18   C. Perkins 2, 3.

19   The cottage home was suggested, probably by Smith in 'This is St Francis House, Semaphore', Centralian Advocate, 2/2/1951.

20   J. Moriarty, interview.

21   G. Briscoe 1.

22 C. Perkins 3.

23 cf. Report of the Northern Territory Committee on Native Welfare: comments and recommendations relating to the welfare and social development of Part-Aboriginals, n.d., c. Oct. 1953, AANT CA 1070 F1 52/250; C. Perkins 4.

24 C. Perkins 3, 4; the Hampton case was a minor *cause célèbre* for opponents of the SA *Aborigines Protection Act*, reported in the press 24/4/1955; for Hampton's account see Mattingley and Hampton 1988. 'Balts' was the name given to the first of 200,000 Displaced Persons who came to Australia between 1947–51. Recent evidence suggests that the 'DPs' were not nearly so well accepted as Perkins imagined.

25 P. Smith, 'Half Caste Training', *ABM Review*, xxii/8, August 1945, pp. 123–4. Smith's contemporaries, even within the church, were often much more racist than Smith; cf. *ABM Review*, xliii/8, 18/1955, pp. 113–14; an editorial praising Smith's work at St Francis remarked with satisfaction 'Our little problem is made much easier by the fact that where there is intermarriage the darker colour breeds right out in a few generations'. The achievements of the boys were noted in *Advertiser*, 8/10/1979.

26 C. Perkins 3.

27 The 'stock reply' was recorded at a St Francis House reunion, *Advertiser*, 8/10/1979. The suggestion that Perkins might have become a traditional healer was made by one of his St Francis House contemporaries.

28 Perkins 1975, p. 31.

29 For example see Bowden and Bunbury 1990; Edwards and Read 1989

Chapter 7 Calling in the accounts

1 Midway though the HREOC enquiry (in April 1996), I was

commissioned to prepare an options paper for the Aboriginal and Torres Strait Islander Commission. I was to investigate any national and international covenants relating to the rights of children relevant to compensating the Stolen Generations. The scope was to be as wide as possible but I should consider the practical pros and cons of any compensation measure which I suggested (Read 1996a). These the ATSIC Commissioners might take into account in preparing their own formal submission to the enquiry. Some of my proposals were incorporated in ATSIC's submission, and a shorter version reprinted as its Appendix C, pp. 39–42. The later section in this chapter drawn from that submission is a shorter and simplified version of the original. The first part of the chapter is drawn from other submissions to courts determining custody and other matters relating to Aboriginal children.

2 HREOC 1997 Appendix 9, pp. 651–665
3 Aborigines Protection Board, Annual Report, 1921–22, p. 2.
4 Circular to Station Managers, 13 September 1922, 'Copies of letters sent', NSW State Archives.
5 'Aborigines race dying out. Fate of girls few chances for marriage', *Sydney Morning Herald*, 29 October 1924.
6 ibid.
7 Aborigines Protection Board, Annual Report, 1925–26, p. 3.
8 Aborigines Protection Board, Minutes of Meetings, 27 February 1927.
9 Aborigines Protection Board, Minutes of Meetings, 27 February 1927.
10 Read 1988 p. 69
11 Discussion and Recommendations following the Departmental Report, Aborigines Protection Board, Minutes of Meetings, 4 December 1935, 4 March 1936.
12 ibid.
13 *Dawn* 1953 (December), p. 13.
14 University of Limburg, Maastricht Human Rights Project Group,

'Seminar on the right to restitution, compensation and rehabilitation for victims of gross violations of human rights and fundamental freedoms', Netherlands Institute for Human Rights, 1992, pp. 17–21.

15 Final Report by Special Rapporteur van Boven, 'Study concerning the right to restitution . . .', UN Sub-Commission on Prevention of Discrimination and Protection of Minorities, 1993, p. 9.

16 Wootton 1989, p. 20.

17 Summerlad 1976.

18 Notes supplied by Gabrielle Hyslop, Exhibitions Officer, Australian Archives.

Chapter 8 Sorry Business

1 This chapter is an expanded version of an article first published in 1998 in the electronic journal *Mots pluriels*.

2 Senator John Herron, Media Release, Canberra, 16 December 1997

3 Quoted by Markus 1990 p. 177, in HREOC, p. 45.

4 Quoted by Gungil Jindibah Centre 1994, p. 44, quoted in HREOC, p. 45.

5 For details of women's activism see Lake 1998, pp. 91–108. I thank Tikka Wilson for her valuable insights in these and other matters discussed in this chapter.

6 The ten points were published in the first issue of *Abo Call*, April 1938. For details of correspondence see Goodall 1996, pp. 188–9.

7 The Victorian Koori Margaret Tucker is the exception; see her autobiography Tucker 1977.

8 I owe this suggestion to Dr Bain Attwood.

9 *Dawn* [NSW Aborigines Welfare Board magazine] 2/12 (December 1953), p. 13.

10 Curthoys in Gray and Winter 1997, pp. 117–18.

11 K. Gilbert, *Australian*, 26 January 1972, in Rose 1996, p. 193.

12 Allen N. Bennett, correspondent in *Advertiser*, 6 February 1998.

13 ibid.

14 ibid.

15 Aborigines Protection Board, NSW, *Annual Report*, 1921.

16 J.M. Drew, Western Australia Parliamentary debates, 1904, quoted by Biskup 1973, p. 142, in HREOC, p. 103.

17 Chief Protector Cecil Cook, quoted Marcus 1990, p. 93, in HREOC, p. 137.

18 J.W. Bleakley, Chief Protector and Director of Native Affairs, quoted Kidd 1994 p. 362, in HREOC, p. 73.

19 Director of Native Affairs, Queensland, quoted in Kidd 1994, in HREOC, p. 529.

20 Rev Hagenauer, General Inspector of the Board, 9 September 1897, quoted in Chesterman and Galligan, 'The Citizenship divide in Victorian Aboriginal administration', 1995, p. 20, in HREOC, p. 59.

21 Chief Protector of Aboriginals, August 1932, quoted in HREOC, p. 119.

22 HREOC, p. 148.

23 *Courier Mail*, 5 December 1997, editorial.

24 Minister for Aboriginal Affairs, *SMH*, 17 December 1997.

25 *Queenslander*, 1883, quoted in Kidd, p. 83, in HREOC, p. 71.

26 Archibald Meston, 'Report on the Aboriginals of Queensland', Queensland Government, Brisbane 1896, p. 4, in HREOC, p. 73.

27 W. Bray to Protector of Aborigines April 1941, reproduced in MacDonald and Australian Archives 1995, p. 47.

28 Minister for Aboriginal Affairs, *Australian*, 17 December 1997.

29 J. Devaney 1929, pp. 230–1, quoted in O'Connor 1998, in Kociumbas 1998, p. 249.

30 Frank Devine, 'Bringing the truth back home', *Australian*, 5 March 1998.

31 Cited by Partington 1996, pp. 30–1.

32 Frank Devine, 'Derisory offerings deserve only contempt', *Australian*, 15 January 1998.

33 Confidential evidence 146, HREOC, p. 191.

34 The one-page records were kept between 1916 and 1936. After that date longer files were maintained on each State Ward.

35 Frank Devine, 'Derisory offerings deserve only contempt', *Australian*, 15 January 1998.

36 Quoted in *Canberra Times*, 26 February 1998.

37 *Abo call*, Editorial, June 1938.

38 Father Doncaster at the South Australian Anglican Synod, *West Australian*, 2 February 1998

39 Senator John Herron to Father Frank Brennan, quoted by Manne 1998, p. 55

40 Minister for Aboriginal Affairs, *Advertiser*, 17 December 1997.

41 Quoted by Marcus 1994, in HREOC p. 46.

Chapter 9 In the courts: 'In the middle of the ocean, drowning'

1 This chapter is based on an article I wrote after visiting Melbourne, Florida, to join the team of expert witnesses giving evidence in the case described. The article 'In the middle of the ocean, drowning: Some observations on the trial and sentencing of Russell Moore' was published in *Overland* (Read 1990a). The remarks about the courts' role are drawn from several submissions written on behalf of clients of the NSW Aboriginal Legal Service.

2 For example, G. Macdonald, 'Fighting behaviour among the Wiradjuri', Anthropology Dept, seminar paper, University of Sydney, 1982; A-K Eckermann, 'Group identity and urban Aborigines' in D. Tugby ed. *Aboriginal Identification in Contemporary Australian Society*, AIATSIS 1973; M. Langton, 'Urbanising

Aborigines—the social scientists' great deception', in *Social Alternatives*, 2/2 (August 1981), pp. 16–22.

3   For example, Tucker 1977, Cummings 1990.

4   Wootten 1989, p. 74.

5   How Russell Moore managed to live as a street child in the US for so long is not known, nor were these facts elicited during the trial or the penalty phase hearing.

Index

A Bastard Like Me (autobiography)
139–40, 142, 145
Abo Call (journal) 163, 184
Aboriginal and Torres Strait
Islander Commission 42
Aboriginal child rearing practices 66
Aboriginality, as defined *see*
identity;
pride in 83–4, 96–7,
Aboriginal nation, owing to 162–3
Aboriginal Progressive
Association 184–5
Aborigines Advancement League
168
Aborigines Protection Act (NSW)
28–9, 32, 45, 53–5
Aborigines Protection
Association 167
Aborigines Protection Board
(NSW) 23, 24, 27, 28–9, 30,
45, 50, 52, 87, 183
Aborigines Welfare Board (NSW)
29–30, 35;
criticism of 152–3;
lack of self-criticism 151–4;
powers of 33

absconding 5, 35, 61–2, 200
acceptance into community 67
Adams, Alicia 34–5
adoptions 37–41, 84, 98;
break down in relations
109–10;
successful 183–4;
theory of 200–2
see also Westmacott, Dianne
Adoptions Act (Vic) 192ff
Adoptions Branch 89
alcoholism *see* effects, alcohol
Alice Springs 125–6, 131–2, 139,
152
analysis of removal, by the
victims 147ff.
see also Perkins, Charles
Anglican Church:
and Charles Perkins 135;
experiences of 128;
institutions 1
apology, by federal government
viii, ix, 186–7
apprenticeships 60–1
Archives Office, NSW 46–8, 86–9
Arthur, Jay 49

Ashfield Childrens Home 52
assimilation, of adults 30
assimilation, of children:
    justification 17, 23, 24;
    possibly desired by Aborigines
        184-5;
    reasons for 22, 53, 68-9, 74;
    records of, in NSW 46 ff.;
    reflections on 148-9;
    success stories 42-3;
    in Victoria 202
attitudes of society 40, 41, 60,
    180-1
Australian Board of Missions
    133-4

Barwick, Diane 115-16
Between Two Worlds (exhibition)
    157-8
Blair, Harold (singer) 8
blood *see* identity
Bloomfield Mental Hospital 12, 52
Board for the Protection of
    Aborigines (Vic) 199-203
Bomaderry Home, NSW 6, 51
Boystown Home x, 10
Bray, Laurie 134
Bringing Them Home (Report)
    150-1, 178-9, 182
Briscoe, Gordon 126, 127, 131-2,
    134, 168, 173, 174, 177-8, 179
'Brown Skin Baby' *see* Randall,
    Bob
Brungle Aboriginal Station 103
Brunton, Dr Ron 166
Bungalow, the, NT 23
Burnside Home 40

Catholic Church 1 *see also* Snake
    Bay

Callan Park Mental Hospital 12,
    15, 178
Cameron, Veronica 1, 2-3
capital punishment (USA) 187,
    189, 192, 204
Carrolup, WA 23
Charles Perkins A Biography 143ff.;
    amendments to the draft of
        145-6
Charcoal Lane, Melbourne xi
Cherbourg, Qld 23
Child Welfare Act, NSW 55
Christmas 96
Churches' role 176-8
    see also Anglican, Catholic
Coe, Agnes 9
Coe, Paul, Snr 9, 32
Colebrook Home, SA x, 23, 131
committal procedures 188-191
commonwealth government,
    responsibility 186-7, 210
    see also apology
comparison to Japan's apology for
    WWII 187
compensation 146, 160-1
contacts with family, preliminary
    88-9
Coombs, Nugget 101
Cooper, Malcolm 120, 123, 134,
    125, 126
Cooper, William 111, 116
Cootamundra Girls Home 2, 10,
    23, 29, 31, 32, 34, 37, 54, 59,
    72, 104, 183, 196
Copley, Vince 125, 130, 133,
    134, 136, 141
court orders 188-91
Cowra NSW 33, 175-6 *see also*
    Erambie
criticism, of institutions 67

see also Perkins, Charles
Crown St Womens Hospital 90
Cruse, Ossie 71
Cumeroongunja station 114–15, 148
Curthoys, Ann 170

Davis, Jack 44–5
Dawn (magazine) 154
de-culturation, examples of 2, 4, 11, 34, 42
Delgado, John 187–90, 192, 194–6, 202
denial of identity see effects, psychological
Devaney, J. 180–1
discovering information 74–5
    see also archives
'disposal' of state ward 182–3
dog-tag, (identity certificate) 33
Donaldson, Inspector 32
Doolan, Flo 33–4
Dyer, Molly 207

education:
    of Charles Perkins 129–130;
    ironical effects of 40–1;
    of the officials 179–80
    see also Cootamundra, Kinchela
Edwards, Coral 48, 70–2, 101
Edwards, Isabel 32
effects of institutionalisation:
    alcohol 52, 67;
    criminal behaviour 43, 191ff;
    drug dependence 8;
    loneliness 35;
    long term 7–9, 11–13, 42ff, 64–5, 107;
    loss of family 43;
    physical 10, 13;

psychological 4, 34, 58–9, 76;
    self-hatred 44, 57;
    shame 106–7;
    summary 159, 203–4
electric shock treatment 12–13
Elkin, A.P. 65–6
employment of wards see institutions, training
Erambie Station, Cowra 2, 12, 31, 32
    see also Wedge, Aileen
Espie, Bill 125, 131–3, 141
expert witnesses 194–7

Family and Childrens Service Agency 49
Fannie Bay xi
Federal Council for the Advancement of Aboriginal and Torres Strait Islanders 170
Ferguson, William 185, 187
files, on wards in NSW see Archives
first trip home, see reunions
forced separation, examples of 24–5
forgiveness viii, 70, 147–8
foster parents 43, 47, 84, 179, 186
    see also parents, 'white'
'full-blood' see full descent Aboriginals
full descent Aboriginals 20–21
    see also Westmacott, Dianne

generations of separations 13–14
genocide 49, 150, 167
Gilbert, Kevin ii, 166, 171, 186, 191
Gunther, James 18–19, 20

Hagenauer, Rev 173, 178
half-castes, parents of 21, 131–2,
    172–3, 174–5
    see also part-Aboriginal
hatred, of officials 148, 180
Hampton, Cyril 138
Herron, John, Senator 161, 166
Human Rights and Equal
    Opportunity Commission
    (HREOC) Enquiry viii, 145,
    150ff, 173, 177, 182;
    response by Federal
        Government 166–7

identity:
    and teacher training 44;
    by skin colouring 21, 67;
    concealing 37;
    definitions of 17–18, 20–2;
    ignorance of 82–3;
    self- 21–22, 26–7, 73–4, 83–4;
    trying to find x–xi, 95–7
    see also Westmacott, Dianne
Ingram, Mrs Louisa 5–6
institutional life:
    abuse 11, 81, 153–4;
    food 2;
    lack of amenities 36;
    lack of training 36–7;
    parental visits 10;
    proportion of Aboriginal
        children in 99;
    punishments 7, 10, 23–4,
        35–6, 68;
    training 59;
    work 3
institutions, examples of 23, 32
intelligence 59–60, 168–70,
    173–4

'John':
    growing up 78;
    hearing the news 75–6, 91;
    returning home 92
judicial procedures see court orders

Kensington Park (Adelaide
    suburb) 126ff.
Kinchela Aboriginal Boys Home
    x, 10, 23, 29, 32, 35–7, 44,
    54–5, 57–9, 68, 72, 139, 148,
    153–4, 196
King, Jane 101ff.;
    at Cootamundra x, 96–102,
        104;
    found in Sydney 106;
    reasons for committal 102–3
Kingsley-Strack, Joan 99, 100,
    104–5

La Perouse 66
leadership, effects on viii
Le Fevre school, Adelaide 129
legislation:
    effects of court orders 188–9;
    NSW 53–6;
    NT 21–22, 27ff., 128, 177;
    Qld 177–9;
    SA 22;
    Vic 178, 192, 200–1;
    WA 22, 177
lesbians 14
Link-Up NSW 65, 70ff.;
    accompanying clients home
        92–5;
    advice on meeting family 78;
    idea for 70;
    funding 71–2, 163;
    helping clients 72ff., 100,
        103ff.;

needing community help 99
Long Bay prison 13–14
Lutanda Home (Plymouth
    Brethren) 6–7

Maastricht Seminar 155–6
marriages, mixed 188–9
'Mary', return to community 74,
    101
Maynard, Fred 15, 162, 167–8
mental health 9–10, 10–11, 15,
    148, 178, 198–9
Methodist Church home 200
missing persons 84–5
missionaries:
    at St Francis House, Adelaide
        127ff.
    see also churches and
        individual denominations
Mittagong State Home x, 32
Morgan, Gladys 181
Moore River settlement, WA x,
    23–4
Moore, Russell x, 44, 191ff
Moriarty, John 13, 125, 126,
    130–1, 134, 136–7
mothers 176;
    in hospitals 78
Mt Margaret, WA 23
Mt Penang institution 32, 55
Mulgoa 130
Musgrave Park xi

Namatjira, Albert 7
Narrandera 175–6
National Aboriginal Consultative
    Committee 71–2
national mythology—as battlers
    170

natural parents, relations with
    92–8, 119ff., 172
Nean, Clarrie x, 36, 44
Neglected Children and Juvenile
    Offenders Act, NSW 28–9, 32,
    53
Nelson, Topsy Napurrula 1, 3–5
New South Wales see legislation,
    numbers
non-Aboriginal children,
    treatment compared 55–6
North Ryde Mental Hospital 8–9,
    12, 13, 15
Northern Territory 21–2
    see also legislation
numbers, of removals:
    Australia 25–6;
    New South Wales 27, 67, 73;
    Victoria 201;
    Wiradjuri country 31–2

O'Donoghue, Lowitja [Lois] 42,
    124
Old Maria 115
Orana Children's Home
    (Methodist) 195
oral history 172, 181
orphans 183–4

Palm Island, Qld 23
parents of removed children 24;
    asking for their children to be
        cared for 176
parents, 'white' 37ff.;
    and capacity to help adopted
        children 38–9, 204–5;
    explanations to 84;
    need for apology 186–7;
    negative attitudes 39

Parkerville, WA (institution) 176, 181

part-Aboriginal 20–2, 30

Parramatta Girls Reformatory 11, 12, 14–15, 55

Parramatta Industrial Home 56

Parramatta Mental Hospital 100

past standards, determining 170–1

Perkins, Charles 43, 124ff.;
  at Le Fevre High School 129–130;
  leaving Alice Springs 125–6;
  physically abused 134;
  reflections on his separation 140–3;
  returning to Alice Springs 131–2

Perkins, Hetti 120, 126, 131–2, 133, 135, 140–1

Phillip, Governor Arthur 17

Phillip Creek 1

Point Pearce Mission, SA 125

policy see legislation, assimilation

prejudice see attitudes of society

protest at separation policy 69, 157, 179–80;
  lack of protest discussed 167, 169, 172

psychological changes:
  negative self image 2, 10–11, 34–5
  see also effects

puberty, of wards 60, 64

public reaction see protest

punishments in institutions see institutions

quadroons 22, 75

Queenslander (newspaper) 179

Randall, Bob 25

records (NSW) 88–90:
  establishing indigenous offices 162;
  in hospitals 90
  see also Archives

Register of Wards, NSW 55, 88, 183
  see also Archives

regulations on reserves see Aborigines Welfare Board, powers of

religious instruction 6
  see also institutions, Church denominations

relinquishing parents see natural parents

removals, reasons for 27–31, 66, 68–9, 75, 98, 149, 162, 165, 166–7, 171, 172–3, 180, 194;
  as punishment 32;
  discussed with Link-Up clients 75;
  need for mothering 154;
  poor health 175;
  subterfuge 77

reparation 145, 153ff.;
  cultural awareness 150, 156–7, 161–2
  land 150, 156, 159–60;
  pension 150, 155, 160;
  principles 145, 153–4, 158

Retta Dixon Home x

returning to communities and families 56, 64–5, 65–6, 92–5, 95–6, 126–7, 198–9;
  after adoption 204;
  difficulties in 101–2, 122–3;
  not returning, discussed 79–81
  see also Link-Up

reunions 64–5, 91–6, 205–7
Roach, Archie 43–4
Roberts, Hagar 24
Roeburn, WA 23
roll of honour 164
Roper River mission (NT) 1, 24
Royal Commission into
    Aboriginal Deaths in Custody
    36, 151, 156, 185

Savage, Graeme and Nesta 193,
    208
Savage, James see Moore, Russell
schooling see education
separations, forced 18–20, 24–5,
    55–6;
    becoming structural 169;
    justified by poor housing
    185–6;
    successful outcomes 183
sexual 'deviation' at Kinchela 58,
    68
Smith, Malcolm 44
Smith, Revd Percy 120ff., 135–8,
    139–44, 144–5, 148
Snake Bay 1, 3
Sorry Day 164
sorry place 159, 164
St Anthony's Home, Sydney 9
St Francis House, Adelaide
    (institution) 120, 123–5,
    126ff., 139;
    deterioration at 133–4
standards of the past 179–80
    see also institutions
State Childrens Council (SA):
state wards 46, 61;
    acquiring a ward 62–3
statistics see numbers

'stolen generations' vii–viii,
    18–19;
    origin of phrase 49;
    original article 49–70;
    records of, as state wards 46–9;
    typical case-history 50–2
    see also Perkins, Charles

The Lost Children (oral history)
    38, 40
The Vanished Tribes 175
Topsy Nelson see Nelson, Topsy
    Napurrula
training courses 161–2
truancy 64–5
    see also absconding
trust fund, establishment of 165
Tucker, Margaret 68

UN Sub-Commission on Prevention
    of Discrimination and Protection
    of Minorities 155–6
Universal Declaration of Human
    Rights 154–5
US criminal procedures 191–2

values, indigenous 189
Van Boven, Special UN
    Rapporteur 156
Victorian Aboriginal Legal
    Service 186, 188, 191, 193
Victorian Aborigines Protection
    Board 173
Victorian Aborigines Welfare
    Board 187, 195, 198–202
violence see effects, criminal
    behaviour

Wagga Base Hospital 112–13
Walgett police station 36

Warangesda mission 28, 31, 53, 54
wardship, end of period *see*
    disposal
Waterfall Sanitarium 51
Watson, William 18–19, 20
Wedge, Aileen 2, 9–16
Wellington Valley mission, NSW
    18–20
Westmacott, Dianne 96, 103ff.;
    childhood 108–9;
    discovery of adoption 110;
    discovery of identity 112–13,
        114–17;
    meeting mother 118–121;

reflections on her search
    121–2;
relationship with adopting
    father 109
Whyman, Beverly 187, 189, 192,
    194, 199ff., 204, 209
Whyman, Frank 187, 191, 192
Williams, Joy x, 2, 5–9, 29–30
Wilson, Sir Ronald 145, 150
Wiradjuri people 18–20, 31ff., 45
Women of the Sun (film) 83
Woorabinda, Qld 23
Wootten, Commissioner Hal 185,
    190–2, 195

Printed in the United States
by Baker & Taylor Publisher Services